C000192889

GUIDE TO
TENNIS

DAVE WHITEHEAD

© Haynes Publishing 2019
Published May 2019

A CIP Catalogue record for this book
is available from the British Library.

ISBN: 978 1 78521 582 7 (print)
        978 1 78521 629 9 (eBook)

Library of Congress control no. 2019930110

Published by Haynes Publishing,
Sparkford, Yeovil, Somerset BA22 7JJ
Tel: 01963 440635
Int. tel: +44 1963 440635
Website: www.haynes.com

Printed in Malaysia.

Series Editor: David Allsop.

CONTENTS

The major tournaments at the time banned the greedy pros because they seemed to possess all the moral backbone of a filleted rabbit.

TENNIS GENESIS

It's a demonstrable fact that most tennis players are people, and that most people are humans. Furthermore, humans have all sorts of failings. These failings are called 'human failings'. Which is good, because nobody wants to go around with hamster failings.

Two of the most prevalent of these human failings are greed and hyperbole. Both are particularly present in athletic competitions, which of course include the game of tennis. Studies indicate that more and more people are becoming prone to describing their achievements, athletic and otherwise, in the most glowing and grandiose terms. In their vaulting ambition to be better than their friends and neighbours at everything from dog grooming to eighteenth-century French literature, people constantly overstate their abilities. Indeed, these descriptions are similar to Hercules: very heroic, but undeniably mythical.

Tennis players are not immune to these failings. Far from it. In fact, if you were to get bored and wander onto an online tennis forum, you would be amazed at how many 'players' say something along the lines of:

'I have no problem hitting winners off my forehand and backhand wings, but every time I try to volley, the ball either gets wedged in my racquet's throat or hits me in the eye.'

This sort of statement sends red flags up to tennis aficionados. If the player is getting hit in the eye, he or she is clearly not very good. Not only that, but said player probably chooses to play exclusively people on crutches, the only opponents against whom he or she can possibly hit winners.

To become the armchair expert at tennis you deserve to be, the particular human skill known as 'bluffing' should be harnessed. Claim it. Embrace it. Own it. As a result, you will be able to impress total strangers with your command of the vast array of tennis facts and minutiae that the sport and this guide provide. You will be able to walk from tennis venue to tennis venue, confident and sure of your ability to hold up your end of semi-profound tennis discussions. For example, when passing by the Royal Box at Wimbledon and the Duke of Yorkshire Pudding enquires, 'I say, my good citizen, do you happen to know if these chaps are on serve?', you will not only know what the hell he's talking about, but you will also know how to answer him without being escorted from the premises by the royal henchmen at the behest of the royal factotum.

But before you do anything else – before you even consider opening your mouth and venturing an opinion on this hallowed game of skill and athleticism – you're going to need a crash course in tennis history. So take a deep breath and strap yourself in. Tennis history won't ever get any shorter than this...

In the beginning... Oh, never mind. Nobody cares. But some say that the game began in France in the fourteenth century, albeit without racquets. So it was more like 'patball' than tennis, and it evolved into another precursor of the modern game called 'royal tennis' (after the French word *tenez* – which means 'hold' or 'here you are', not that this really helps). Apparently it was popular at the court of Henry VIII, and subsequently became known as 'real tennis', which never really took off because the indoor courts were so expensive to build. Ultimately, the game became 'lawn tennis' and only a nerdy tennis historian or a citizen of England's reputed second city would know the following titbit of tennis trivia.

The modern game can be traced back to 1860 in Birmingham. Apparently, they had a lot of free time in this Midlands manufacturing powerhouse, which later became the birthplace of heavy metal music (Led Zeppelin, Black Sabbath, Judas Priest), not to mention The Move, ELO, The Moody Blues and a few more. This is all vital bluffing information, but back to tennis history. In those days there weren't quite so many opportunities to let your hair down and 'headbang', and what with most women walking around in conservative Victorian garb back then, it is safe to assume that men would have spent a lot of time wildly imagining a game which at some point in the future might involve the fairer sex wearing noticeably shorter skirts. So they invented a primitive form of tennis, played on a lawn.

All you need to know is that a couple of young Birmingham blades, one called Major Harry Gem and the other with the unmistakeably Brummie name of Juan Bautista Luis Augurio Perera, met in a pub called the Welch Harp and agreed that there wasn't a suitable sport which could be played by both sexes and which involved women wearing rather fewer clothes than was then considered acceptable. Actually, the history of their exact conversation is a little hazy, but it is safe to assume that it was something along those lines. So Harry and Juan (who was a Spanish-born entrepreneur) set about inventing lawn tennis. This is absolutely true. And the Welch Harp became better known as the now sadly defunct Racquet Court Inn.

This knowledge may be useful in conversations in pubs to indicate that you are either a tennis nerd or from Birmingham. Perhaps after a couple of pints with your friends, when the subject has turned to the weather, you can say:

> **You** Birmingham has more miles of canal than Venice.
> **Friend** How extraordinary.
> **You** And not only that, Birmingham is the birthplace of modern tennis!

Just don't be surprised when the pub landlord shows you and your friends the door after relieving you of your car keys.

A whole lot of historic things have happened in Birmingham between then and now. Most, like canals, the industrial revolution, gunmaking, inventions, jewellery, heavy metal music, more canals, etc., did not concern tennis. So it's time to jump ahead to an even more modern tennis history.

From its beginnings in Victorian Birmingham to well into the next century, tennis players were divided into two main groups – non-paid amateurs and paid professionals. The amateurs played for the love of the sport (and doubtless some under-the-table hard cash). As for the pros, getting paid over the table to play tennis was considered to be cheap and seedy. Therefore only players of high moral fibre played top levels of tennis for 'free'. The major tournaments at the time (e.g., Wimbledon) banned the greedy pros because they seemed to possess all the moral backbone of a filleted rabbit.

Only players of high
moral fibre played top levels
of tennis for 'free'.

Then the turbulent 1960s happened and people began to question the existing cultural mores. 'What the hell is it with all these cultural mores?' they would ask. At the same time (actually, over the course of many years), people started thinking 'free love' (aka 'no-strings sex') was a better cultural more than most existing ones.

In 1968 the tennis world turned upside down. The prestigious major tournaments were opened to the pros, and it was immediately decreed by tennis pundits the world over to be the beginning of tennis's 'Open Era'. Those same tennis pundits then wondered what the era before the Open Era should be called. Some pundits thought it should be the 'Closed Era'.

Frankly, it's surprising that when trying to come up with a clever name those pundits didn't tap into whatever mind-altering substance the inventors of tennis's hare-brained scoring system used. Instead, they came up with: 'Before the Open Era'. Brilliant.

You are now sufficiently well versed in the development of the game of tennis to venture an opinion on how and when it all started. But there's a lot more to it than that, as you're about to discover. Many a hidden peril lies in wait for the unsuspecting novice preparing to dip a toe into the turbulent waters of tennis debate.

This short but definitive guide will therefore conduct you through the main danger zones encountered in discussions about the game of tennis and will equip you with a vocabulary and evasive technique that will minimise the risk of being rumbled as a bluffer. It will give you a few easy-to-learn hints and nuggets of essential information that might even allow you to be accepted as a tennis expert of rare ability and experience. But it will do more. It will give you the tools to impress legions of marvelling listeners with your forensic knowledge of the game, and your skill at playing it – without anyone discovering that, until you read it, you didn't know the difference between tennis elbow and a housemaid's knee.

GETTING IN GEAR

Before you get anywhere near a court, you'll need to know how to look the part. Tennis, like ballet, fishing, motorcycling and hang-gliding, needs specialised gear. And, in theory, the more expensive it is, the better your performance. You should spare no expense when reciting what comprises your imaginary kitbag.

WHAT A RACQUET

The number-one item you need to say you have is a racquet. From their modest wooden beginnings, racquets have become remarkable objects of advanced engineering. Every racquet manufacturer retains teams of scientists and engineers who work to develop ever more advanced racquet technologies.

These dedicated and brilliant minds create racquets from space-age materials such as titanium, molybdenum, thorium and delirium, and today's models come in various forms of non-dietary fibre. There are Kevlar fibres, graphite fibres, glass fibres (or fibreglass if you prefer), intellifibers and even plant fibres (they don't say which plant, so you're safe in assuming that it's probably hemp). Somehow, according to some of these same engineers, fibres affect how a tennis ball flies. Note that, unlike the fibre you eat, they have nothing to do with easing constipation.

Other advances at play in modern racquet technology include liquid metal, magnets, boron and strategic holes. You only need to remember these when you're in the company of tennis geeks (and you really should try to avoid this sort of company). This technology is intended to give the player either more power, more spin, more control or any combination thereof. It goes without saying, but say it anyway: most tennis players would play the same way whether they used a racquet manufactured using the latest technology or a shovel.

The pros get their racquets by the container-load from the various racquet companies. Everyone else has to get theirs at retail outlets, where earnest young salespeople in pleated shorts apply the latest selling techniques to get you to buy something you neither want nor need. But having made a purchase, you should claim to own at least two racquets of the same brand and model, one of which you actually play with. The entirely imaginary 'other' is the one you use when your main one is in the pro shop for string repairs. You might consider selecting your real and imaginary racquets from one of the following leading manufacturers:

* Wilson
* Babolat
* Head
* Prince

There are about 20 models for each brand, so instead of memorising one, just tell inquisitive people that the racquet you chose 'felt good' in your hand. That's all you need to say.

Note that there is a valuable old bluff which you can always call on if you want to make a statement on a tennis court. That statement is: 'I know I'm going to lose and I don't care. I'm a Corinthian by nature, and it's the taking part that counts.' The best way of making this statement is to choose to play with an ancient, pre-graphite racquet. A good example is something like a 1960s wooden Dunlop Matchpoint, with one of those wooden stretchers with wing nuts on each corner. About £24 on eBay. Slazenger has a good range of antediluvian racquets as well. People will probably pay to watch you play.

RACQUET HEAD SIZE

You may be asked for your racquet head size. Just say mid-size. Only a great player or an ignorant hack would play with a smaller head size. Only a bad bluffer would play with a larger one. It doesn't make it any easier to hit the ball (actually it does, but there's no guarantee it will land in your opponent's court).

GRIP SIZE

This is the circumference of the racquet's handle. If the subject comes up talk about the importance of 'effective power transfer' via the right size of grip. Then find one that feels comfortable.

OVERGRIPS

Overgrips are thin and tacky grip covers, and good things to claim to be aware of (as in: 'Damn, forgot to pack my overgrips'). If a player doesn't use one, the base grip will eventually lose all tackiness and begin to slip in his or her hand. Players don't like grips that slip, so they use overgrips and toss them out like used cat litter when they wear out.

STRING THEORY

Tennis strings are now as high-tech as racquets. Players can still use good old gut, made out of animal intestine (the most resilient material for strings), but that's not what the pros use. So, be like most players and use something as modern as polyester, which (you will say) provides 'increased topspin'. Players have nicknamed these strings 'polys'. Polyester was invented in 1941 by British scientists John Whinfield and James Dickson. It is one of Britain's few contributions to lawn tennis (apart from inventing it).

Amazingly, the primary string manufacturers are the same as the racquet manufacturers. Nevertheless, be sure to select a different manufacturer from your racquet manufacturer. It demonstrates that you have given some (hopefully) reasoned thought to your decision. If asked why, just say your brand gives 'more feel'. 'More feel' is so personal that, like 'felt good' (*see* page 13), everyone will accept it.

A useful bluffing note is that although it is frequently

known as 'catgut', the vast majority of animal gut strings are made from cowgut.

BAGS

Tennis players need to tote their gear from place to place. They tend to use tennis bags and/or a lackey for this purpose. You can generally tell a tennis bag from a regular bag because it more or less resembles the shape of a large tennis racquet and the manufacturer's name will be printed so large it can be read from passing aircraft.

As a general rule from a bluffing point of view, the bigger the bag you carry, the better the player you are.

As a general rule from a bluffing point of view, the bigger the bag you carry, the better the player you are. The better players require bigger bags because of all the stuff they carry: multiple racquets, sweatbands, sunglasses, hats, socks, towels, sports drinks, lottery tickets, Viagra, voodoo dolls and soap-on-a-rope.

In fact, your tennis bag should have shoulder straps, like a backpack. A great bluffer will sling a vast bag over his or her shoulders like a Sherpa and head out for the court with jaws clamped and an air of Zen-like focus. If first impressions count for anything, your opponent will be ready to concede the moment you unzip your impressive appendage.

BALLS

It takes balls to play tennis. The minimum number of balls that tennis players play with is called a 'can'. (Most cans contain three balls.) Players use all three at a time. You are allowed to use two balls if you have hit one over a fence and into the backyard of a house with a slavering dog at the end of a chain.

Better (and better-funded) players will use two cans of balls at once. In this way, the balls stay 'fuzzy' – meaning good – longer and there's always a ball nearby to pick up and hit. Bluffers should follow their example.

ATTIRE

People have been wearing various forms of purpose-designed tennis attire since Harry and Juan started batting a ball back and forth in Birmingham wearing long white flannels and boaters.

Female players of that day wore the feminine equivalent: long dresses with hemlines down to the alluring feminine ankle, usually concealed beneath black-laced ankle boots in case male spectators should see a titillating flash of fibula. Then there were the mandatory two or three stiff petticoats as well as bustles and corsets, not to mention full bonnets tied with a scarf. It's amazing that they didn't self-combust.

At some point since then, fashion design became an actual career path instead of a hobby. Those career fashionistas subsequently made a thorough study of women's legs and correctly concluded that tennis dresses weren't short enough. The tennis-playing public eagerly agreed. Fashion designers colluded and very quickly all hemlines rose like vampires' coffin lids in the night.

At around the same time, men's fashion lurched toward short sleeves and shorts. The tennis-playing public were largely indifferent. 'So?' they yawned.

For some reason (probably to do with Wimbledon), tennis clothing designers could only secure white fabric. Therefore, tennis as a sport became synonymous with white: white shirts, white dresses, white shorts, white socks, white shoes, white balls, even white players and spectators.

Then, in the mid-1970s, a tennis clothing designer discovered a roll of yellow cloth. Immediately, he was struck by a bolt of inspiration. 'What would happen', he mused, 'if tennis players were to wear something other than white?'

The rest is tennis history. Colour exploded onto the tennis scene like a direct hit on a paintball factory – confined, at first, to the pastels section. When the tennis pundits didn't complain about those Easter-egg colours, designers tried bolder ones, like black. Today, colours are as ubiquitous on tennis attire as double-glazing salesmen on the end of your phone. Except at Wimbledon (see page 21).

You should also be aware of the most prominent tennis clothing manufacturers. These are the biggies. They're the ones who pay the pros gazillions to wear their fashions. They are also the ones you need to say you wear. Any of the following will do:

* Nike
* Adidas
* Sergio Tacchini
* Uniqlo
* Lacoste

If you want to push your luck, you could say you wear a different brand, but only if you say the owner is a friend.

SHOES

The clothing manufacturers also generally make the shoes. As a general rule, there should be two of them, unless you are playing a dangerous bluff by deliberately handing your opponent an advantage.

Try to avoid wearing anything that squeaks or has soles with flashing lights. Your shoes should be both understated and functional. If asked, say that you chose them for their 'Zelcron cushioning', 'Adapttrex mould' and 'breathable vamp' (deliberately perforated upper). None of this means anything but it sounds good. They should also fit comfortably, because tennis and blisters are not happy bedfellows. Finally, ensure that they have none of the following written on them: 'turbo', 'precision', 'performance', 'power' – not least because none of these bold claims are likely to be reflected in your play.

WARM-UPS

Unless it's very hot, professional tennis players wear

warm-up suits. Of course, they have a very compelling reason to wear them, mainly that they're paid to (a nice gig if you can get it). You don't need to strain yourself guessing which companies make them; go to the attire list and pick one.

SWEATBANDS AND HEADBANDS

Some players wear sweatbands on their wrists, and headbands on their heads, because they perspire heavily. The musclebound Mallorcan Rafa Nadal is a notable perspirer, although he tends to favour a dashing piratical bandana to absorb perspiration rather than an elasticated band. Many pros wear a variety of these accessories to soak up sweat running down their foreheads into their eyes*, even though they have people loitering around the court ready to hand them towels after every point. Do not claim to have such an entourage, because they're expensive. For the record: an entourage is a group of people, each of whom provides a particular service for a given individual. One keeps track of the money. One does the shopping. One sees to dietary needs. One arranges social activities. Another drives them around. Amazingly, at one time, everybody had one. She was called 'mum'.

---

* It has become something of a tradition for winners of major tennis matches to throw their head and wristbands into the crowd. These damp and malodorous keepsakes are much prized for some indiscernible reason.

HATS AND CAPS

Hats worn by players on a tennis court serve a number of purposes:

- if they have a peak they act as a useful sun shield and can be worn backwards or sideways in the style of recalcitrant teenagers or sulking superbrats. (Not a great look.)
- they can reduce the effects of sunstroke and glare
- they can be useful in soaking up that pesky head sweat (assuming that you ever run around enough to produce it)
- they are also useful as something to throw to the ground in a tantrum (as yet there is no such misdemeanour known as 'hat abuse')

Unlike a baseball cap there is no such thing as a definitive tennis hat, and it would be unwise to borrow any headcovering associated with any other sport, such as a swimming cap, a rugby scrum cap, a cricket helmet, or a top hat (fox hunting). Your best bet is to wear something understated which has a peak and an adjustable fastening. If you're Australian you can be forgiven for opting for the Foreign Legion look with a neck flap (the sun can be brutal down under). If you're female, resist the temptation to wear something elaborate designed by a milliner, and go for something plain and sensible like the sun visors favoured by Maria Sharapova (although, to be honest, she'd still look good in a novelty Christmas turkey hat).

SUNGLASSES

Professionals don't wear them on court, so neither should you. They're one more thing to worry about when a tennis ball is about to hit you squarely between the eyes.

WIMBLEDON FASHION CODE

Why do players have to wear white at Wimbledon? Because it's tradition, that's why. If it ain't broke, don't fix it. That's the way it's done in Blighty. Now toddle off and stop asking silly questions.

There is a perfectly sensible dress code which comprises ten points, all dealing with the colour white. In brief, Wimbledon competitors must wear suitable tennis attire most of which must be 'totally' white, 'completely' white, or 'almost entirely' white (depending on the clothing or accessory in question). Undergarments must also be white except for a single trim of colour no wider than one centimetre (10mm), and note that 'common standards of decency are required at all times'. Finally, 'medical supports and equipment should be white if possible but may be coloured if absolutely necessary'. So an off-white dressing for a nasty wound sustained by the umpire falling off a chair simply won't do. Somebody will just have to go and find a white one. It couldn't be much clearer really.

*Learning to keep score in tennis
is like learning to make intelligible
the cross-pollinated relationships
in a soap opera.*

WHAT'S THE SCORE?

The first thing a bluffer needs to know about playing the game is how to keep the score properly. It sounds easy enough. However, since the early tennis pioneers couldn't figure out how to count by ones, keeping score isn't as simple as counting to four or five, or whatever. The answers to this mysterious scoring system are shrouded in the foggy past. It's always safe to blame the French in these circumstances; after all, the word 'deuce' sounds like one of theirs.

Before you get into the nuts and bolts of scoring, you should be aware of the following:

A LITTLE SCORING HISTORY

Keeping score is an ancient humanoid rite. Moreover, it is governed by Darwinism. Darwinism says that animals with the biggest, or the mostest, or the bestest whatever will survive to reproduce. As soon as our ancestors figured that out, they quickly invented numbers to keep score, which included the number zero. It's not difficult to imagine:

Neanderthal guy 1 Hey, Goob, I just scored with Barbi down by the communal comfort station.
Neanderthal guy 2 Cool, dude! I just tried it with Dorothy and got a big fat zero!

This easy, linear numerical scoring system worked well for thousands of years. Everyone was happily documenting whatever they needed to keep count of by notching their wooden clubs or bedposts. Then one day, tennis happened.

Various competing tennis groups quickly formed. The linear score faction must have lost the internal battle for scoring-system rights to the nutters who conjured up a system so improbable it is still used today.

The latter were able to transform tennis's simple linear scoring system into a low-grade, verbal Rubik's cube. Gone was the familiar 1, 2, 3, 4 paradigm that players of ping-pong have always contentedly used. Gone was its intuitive nature. In its stead was something far more complex. Now, learning to keep score in tennis is like learning to make intelligible the cross-pollinated relationships in a soap opera.

THE FRENCH CONNECTION

People new to the sport might wonder why the scoring system is so unnecessarily convoluted. Bluffers can advance a possible explanation for this, and it could well be down to the French again. Legend has it that in the early days in France the match score was kept with the help of a clock on a wall of the court (don't forget that it used to be an indoor game). To show the score the hands were moved clockwise in increments of 15 up to the top of the hour.

That doesn't explain why 40 isn't called 45, or 'deuce' 60, but let's not be picky. Just accept that they did things differently in those days.*

GIVING GOOD SCORE

To speak 'tennis' effectively, you will often be called upon to 'give the score'. Genuine tennis fans typically run up after a match and breathlessly blurt: 'Who won?!' That question will always be followed by: 'What was the score?!'

Other times, such as when passing by a tennis court where players are in action, some inexplicably interested person may innocently whisper: 'What's the score?' If that's the case, and they can't be bothered to stay put and pay attention, bat them off with: 'What am I? An umpire?' Or, alternatively, you could really confuse them by replying: '27-11, double advantage deuce.'

Tennis competitions are called matches. Matches are made up of sets, which are made up of games, which are made up of points, which are made up of shots, which are made by players. For a full understanding of the scoring system you must get to grips with the points that constitute a game.

---

* There's also a theory that the word 'love' derives from the French word 'l'oeuf' which means egg, because an egg looks like a zero. Apparently.

ANATOMY OF A GAME

At this point a table may prove helpful. However, mind the asterisks:

	NO OF POINTS	1ST POINT	2ND POINT	3RD POINT	3 POINTS EACH	POINT AFTER DEUCE
FOR SERVER	Love*	15**	30**	40***	Deuce****	Advantage-in
FOR RETURNER	Love*	15**	30**	40***	Deuce****	Advantage-out

* Love-Love or Love-all is never announced. It is silently assumed knowledge.

** 15-15 is always 15-all. 30-30 is always 30-all (and not deuce).

*** 40-40 is always called deuce, never 40-all.

**** Could consist of 4 or more points each.

Bear in mind that the server's score is always announced first. There are a fairly large number of things you are allowed to forget about with only minor repercussions, like parking tickets and wedding anniversaries. But never, ever forget to announce the server's score first. If you forget and your bluff is called for this infraction, plead a flashback due to substance abuse (preferably Class A) as a teen. It's perfectly plausible, and you may even gain a modicum of respect for being someone who found redemption in tennis.

As shown in the scoring table above, deuce means 40-all. However, since tennis is almost always a win-by-two affair, the point after deuce means that either the server or the returner has the advantage (ahead by one). However, having the advantage is not good enough in tennis. The advantage player still must close the deal by winning yet another point.

If the player with the advantage loses the next point, the score returns to deuce. In this way, a single game can last for a considerable time before the win-by-two condition is triggered and a new game commences with the returner acting as the server. That's because players take turns serving. All clear so far?

SETS

Tennis matches almost always consist of winning two out of three sets. There are a couple of exceptions to this that you will need to remember. First, in the major tournaments, called the Grand Slam events, and the Davis Cup (where national teams annually play a single-elimination tournament), men play three out of five sets. Often interminably. Second, tennis clubs and time-pressured tournaments may play a 'pro set'. These are particularly popular in the USA but not so well known in the UK – so they offer valuable bluffing potential (especially when you're claiming to have played your best tennis as a semi-pro in Florida). A pro set means the first player to win eight games and win by two is the winner and earns the right to play again. They are constrained, however, because at 8-8 they play a 12-point tiebreaker. (Fear not, explanation coming.)

In a normal match, the players play sets by repeatedly playing games with each other until one reaches the necessary total of six games. In keeping with the win-by-two tradition, the other player can have won only four games or fewer.

If the players' skills are equally matched, the score

could reach 6-5 or 5-6, depending on who is serving. The winner of the next game either a) wins the set 7-5, or b) makes the score 6-6, and sends the set into a dramatic tiebreaker.

Tiebreakers were invented in the early 1970s by a man with a clear head and possibly a terminal illness.

TIEBREAKERS

Tiebreakers were invented in the early 1970s by a man with a clear head and possibly a terminal illness. He needed to speed things up, so he invented tiebreaking. Without the tiebreaker system, matches could, and actually once did, last for days – yes, precious tournament days. (*See* Pancho Gonzales, page 79, and John Isner and Nicolas Mahut, page 99.)

When the tiebreaker is completed, the winner will have won the set 7-6 (n). The 'n' stands for the number of points won by the loser. You will notice it is not a win-by-two score. Aha, but it secretly is. The tiebreaker is won by the first player to reach seven points and win by two. That's all you really need to know about scoring a tiebreaker, so just concentrate on getting the ball over the net when it's your turn to serve or return.

The tiebreaker begins with the player who would normally have served next after the number of games reached 6-6, serving first. After this first point, the other player gets to serve for the next two points. Then the player who served first gets to serve for the next two points, and so on until they have played six points. Then they switch ends of the court (without sitting down to rest or pout or 'focus'). They then follow the same serve pattern, alternating between deuce and ad courts, for another six points and switch ends again. This pattern continues until the win-by-two condition is met.

Quite clear? Relax. You now know how to score, roughly (which is more than many umpires do).

Interpol could identify individuals based solely on their service motions. Like many crime scenes, yours might not be a pretty sight.

HOW MAY I SERVE?

Serves are the shots that start a point. One player, the server, sets himself or herself up to serve. In fact, they set themselves up to smash the ball past (or preferably into) their wide-eyed trembling opponent. It seems almost unfair.

This is one of tennis's little jokes. You see, most players had (and still have) a hard time hitting their first serves into the service area. This 'Out' syndrome was once so common that players started voicing their displeasure to the venerable rule makers at not being able to actually enjoy a bit of a rally (that's when players hit the ball back and forth more than once each). As they started drifting away from the game on the grounds that it was no fun, the rules were changed to allow the server an extra (slightly less ambitious) attempt at hitting the ball into the required part of the court. That rule proved to be a real hit in Birmingham. Tennis once again became fashionable in elite social circles and eventually found its way to London, from whence it spread throughout the empire like a super-virus.

Since players start each point serving, you will know a serve when you see one – especially when it's executed by a male player. The server will walk up to the baseline (the end of the marked playing area), bounce the ball on the ground a few times, then a few more times, toss the ball into the air, step away because something has distracted him, bounce it a few more times, toss it into the air again, and then, in an overt display of pure testosterone, coil himself into a human slingshot and try to smash that ball into what scientists have identified as 'smithereens'. Time will stand still for a moment, and then the server will usually be seen walking sheepishly out of the court to collect the ball he's just hit into a tree, or approaching the net to remove the ball that didn't quite make it over.

Humbled, he will repeat the same serve preparation. This time, however, instead of a terrifying testosterone-fuelled display, he will 'pat' the ball over with all the force of Brahms's *Lullaby*. Understandably, this feeble effort induces about the same amount of fear and trepidation in the service returner as a light tickle with a feather.

ON SERVE

'On serve' is a scoring term. It is included here because it highlights how the serve is generally viewed.

On serve means that the two opponents have served so very effectively that they have tediously won every game in which they have served. Obviously, you would use the term most often when watching the pros. At club and municipal courts you would be unlikely to use it quite so much.

Just the same, when someone asks you the score, you would respond, for example, that they are on serve at 4-5. That means that the server has four games and the receiver has five. If the server looks likely to win, or 'hold', his or her serve, the two are essentially tied. In a win-by-two sport, it also means that eventually they must enter into a tiebreaker (see page 28).

Incidentally, the term 'on serve' works equally well for the two players who lose every game in which they serve. Complicated? Of course it is! This is tennis.

BROKEN SERVE

If one player has 'broken serve' (won the other player's service game), he is said to be 'up a break'. Accordingly, the other player will be 'down a break'.

BIG SERVE

Serves are the backbone of the 'power game'. What is the power game, you might ask? Beloved of bluffers through the ages, it is, sadly, on the verge of extinction. The power game has been discouraged and downgraded in recent years and is now all but a distant memory.

You see, spectators got bored watching the big servers play on fast courts. A typical game went something like this: serve, miss. Serve, miss. Serve, miss. Serve, miss. Game. This was especially true on the fast, grass courts of Wimbledon. It was not true at all on the slow, clay courts of the French Open at Roland Garros. It seems that when spectators get bored, they tend to do non-profitable things like go home or change the channel or rake some leaves or something – anything – else. Therefore…

The tennis powers decided that tennis needed more and longer rallies. So, they decided to slow down the courts (unofficially and off the record, of course). However, the professional players noticed. They noticed that if they served and volleyed (*see* page 61) in the style of the traditional power game, the returners could now shoot their returns past them like London taxis in the rain.

You can study hours of videos
of Pistol Pete's serve, but you won't
be able to duplicate it.

There are still, quite literally, some very big servers playing the game. Most of them are 6ft 5in or taller. Then again, at that height, they move from place to place on the court with all the speed of an ISP help desk. So, 'holding serve' (winning the game in which they are serving, *see* above) is more difficult for them on slow courts.

And 'breaking serve' against a faster, more agile opponent is more difficult still. So, unsurprisingly, earning a top-10 ranking in the world by relying on a power game is about as likely as becoming fluent in Swahili overnight.

PERSONAL SERVE

Serves are deeply personal things. No two players serve alike. It's true. You could say to yourself: 'Okay, I'm going to serve exactly like Pete Sampras.' That's a noble goal. You can study hours of videos of Pistol Pete's serve, but you won't be able to duplicate it. You may be able to hit the ball as hard as he did (actually, that's unlikely), but your service motion won't look anywhere near his. Your serve will look like you serving. That's because serves are so individualistic – Interpol could identify individuals based solely on their service motions. Like many crime scenes, yours might not be a pretty sight.

SERVICE FACTS

Here are a few service facts you should know:

* You get two serves per point. Unless you're allowed a 'let'.
* A 'let' is when your serve hits the net and goes 'in' the other side of it, and you get another go.
* You begin a service game by serving in the 'deuce' side of the court (the right side for the player).
* You alternate serving in the deuce and ad service courts. This also happens in tiebreakers (*see* page 28).
* Bad serves – those which fail to cross the net or land 'out' on the other side – are called 'faults'.
* Two bad serves in a row are collectively called, not surprisingly, a 'double fault'. You lose the point.
* To serve, take a serve stance and bounce the ball a

few times before serving. It's extremely boring for the player awaiting serve (and everybody else), but it's what every server does.

*   If you step on or across the baseline before you hit the ball, it's a fault – more precisely, a 'foot fault'. Ask Serena Williams about them (from a safe distance).

*   You don't have to serve overarm, but you must use the racquet (note that in other racquet sports, such as badminton and squash, it is obligatory to serve underarm. Otherwise it's a fault.)

*   You don't have to swing your racquet at a 'toss' that you have screwed up. A toss is when you throw the ball in the air to hit it.

*   If you swing at a toss and totally miss, it's a fault and you're a tosser.

TYPES OF SERVE

As you will shortly learn, just about every shot is hit with some sort of controlling spin. The same goes for serves. So, with that in mind, you'll need to know about types of serve.

Flat serve

A flat serve means 'without spin'. That's not entirely accurate. Flat serves still spin, but there's just a whole lot less spin. So, the question is: when do you use a flat serve? Answer: when you are trying to impress impressionable onlookers – or when you are 6ft 10in tall.

It is ill-advised to claim a flat serve as your default serve. Since it is relatively without spin, it is very easy to hit the ball out – which, as you know, is a fault, and not generally a good tactic. But, and here's the bluff, you can claim to hit flat serves sparingly as a strategy to 'keep your opponent guessing'. Nobody likes to be kept guessing – especially service receivers.

Slice serve

The slice serve is the easiest to hit. Anyone can hit it – just not necessarily in the service box. A slice serve is hit on one side of the ball with a tilted racquet face. The ball rolls along the face and starts to spin. The ball curves with the spin. Slice serves can be spun at different serve speeds; the most powerful kind is called a 'power slice'. Claim you hit the power slice.

Topspin serve

Yes, it's possible to hit a topspin serve, though it's not that common. It's on the order of a six o'clock to 12 o'clock brush up the backside of the ball. This serve tends to dive down into the court and then bounce higher than otherwise normal. Performed properly, it forces the returner to move either back or forward, depending how much spin is on it.

Twist serve

The twist serve is hit by brushing up the back of the ball from the seven o'clock to one o'clock position. The ball once again curves with the spin, but then bounces away from the curve instead of moving along it. Tennis hackers get aced by these serves every time because they set up where the curve would take it if it actually did bounce with the curve. But it doesn't. Ha!

SERVICE RETURNS

The shot that players use to return serves is called a 'service return' (or a 'serve return' in the USA). Because service returners have to hit returns as either forehands or backhands, you might wonder why they aren't simply called 'forehands' or 'backhands'. It apparently takes too much of an effort to say 'forehand service return' or 'backhand service return'. So players, spectators and commentators shortened it to the generic 'service return'.

Sometimes there isn't actually any sort of a 'return'. Often, serves come over the net so fast the returner can't even lay a racquet on them. In such cases, the returner is said to have been 'aced'. Aces are an important statistic – so important that tennis nerds keep a careful record of them. You need not.

There are the times when the returner hits his or her return out or into the net for no earthly reason.

Other times, the returner can put his or her racquet on the ball, but is only able to dribble it up to the net. In other words, the server forced an error from the returner with the sort of hypersonic serve that would bring down a wild boar.

Typically, the server's ball is heading at the returner so fast that there isn't time to hit a normal forehand or backhand stroke, and certainly no time to remember the requisite racquet preparation and measured footwork. In those cases, returners must improvise a valiant attempt at a return. Instead, they tend to swipe at the fast-passing balls like a drunk at a passing beer truck. Don't laugh at them when they stumble and flail around the court. Bluffers should never mock the afflicted.

Then there are the times when the returner hits his or her return out or into the net for no earthly reason. Those errors are known as 'unforced errors' and are also highly valued statistics by tennis nerds. Indeed, tennis nerds keep all kinds of statistics. Among them are aces, unforced errors, double faults, points won at the net, winners, first serve percentage and so on. They find these statistics meaningful as, indeed, do tennis commentators who need to fill air time when pro tennis players are enjoying one of their frequent mid-match rests. As a bluffer, there's absolutely no harm in trying to remember some of them.

------------------------------ *ß* ------------------------------

Bluffers don't demonstrate. They suffer from tennis elbow or another similarly calamitous injury that precludes them from demonstrating.

YOUR HOT SHOTS

You will be expected to know a forehand from a backhand, as well as the other shot types. Otherwise, you will immediately exhibit the keen tennis knowledge of a Tunisian dung beetle – which isn't exactly the vibe you're seeking.

FOREHANDS

Forehands, you will claim, are fantastic. At least, that's the consensus of most tennis players who know one end of a tennis racquet from another. It should be your publicly expressed opinion as well, although you can get away with insisting that your serve is your favourite shot as long as you flatly maintain that you can hit the sucker 120 miles per hour. However, if you do express that opinion, be prepared. You'll need to look the part. (A few years of pumping iron will be enough to pull it off.) Otherwise, you may be asked for a demonstration. If so, remember The First Rule of Bluffing:

Rule no 1 (there is only one): Bluffers don't demonstrate. They suffer from tennis elbow or another similarly calamitous injury that precludes them from demonstrating.

A forehand is hit on the same side of your body as your dominant arm. Remember this simple mantra: right for righties; left for lefties. Backhands are hit on the other, weak, non-dominant side (which is why it's not a good idea to claim it's your favourite shot). Another dead giveaway that a shot is a backhand and not a forehand is that the vast majority of all backhands are hit with two hands. This is an affectation which has crept insidiously into the game in the last 30 years or so.

You will need to know that there is more than one type of forehand. It's a necessity, really. This necessity is mainly due to the fact that the opponent is on the other side of the net plotting all sorts of devious and underhand ways to make your return shots as difficult as possible. The low-life swine.

BASIC FOREHANDS

Topspin
Topspin makes the ball drop faster, permitting a higher clearance over the net. It also makes the ball bounce higher and therefore difficult to return with any great power. Players generally use it to keep the ball from flying into the back fence. A topspin forehand makes the ball spin with what tennis hackers call 'overspin'.

Since you don't want to be identified as an ignorant hacker, never use the term 'overspin'. Always say 'topspin'.

Hitting topspin requires the racquet to come from under the ball and up. The ball rolls down the strings, thus imparting the spin. If asked how to produce this spin, you will reply authoritatively that the racquet take-back and forward swing should look similar to the shape of the letter C. If you happen to identify someone executing a take-back and forward swing in the shape of a number two, say confidently that the person shouldn't be on a tennis court. Anyone within earshot will nod in agreement at your profound wisdom and insight.

Slice

A slice forehand makes the ball spin with 'backspin'. Players use it to keep the ball low to their opponent. As you may expect, the racquet comes from above the ball and down in a 'slicing' motion. That's why it's called a slice. The ball rolls up the strings, not down. And the stroke comes down and forward.

You will seldom see this type of forehand actually struck at the higher levels of the game. The topspin variety is almost always the better option for the pros. Still, you will see the slice forehand from time to time from top players who want to confound their opponent. To paraphrase that noted tennis player Winston Churchill: 'Fail to prepare. Prepare to fail.' So be prepared for the slice shot – and especially for the squash shot...

SPECIALITY FOREHANDS

Squash shot

This is a peculiar forehand slice shot that you may see once or twice a match. Only the better players hit it; the rest don't even know it has a name. (It is safe to assume that it is named after some type of squash shot, but you'll have to wait for *The Bluffer's Guide to Squash* to find out.) Regardless, it is a forehand that is hit on a dead run or when caught moving in the wrong direction. The player hitting it will raise his or her racquet overhead and then, at the last moment as the ball passes, reach out toward the side fence and chop at the ball before it gets by. Somehow physics works its magic and the ball sometimes stays in play.

Reverse forehand

This is also sometimes called a 'bolo' forehand. The reverse forehand doesn't actually reverse anything. No one knows why it is called a 'reverse' forehand. Indeed, its origin is muddied (probably on purpose by the rule makers). The only thing we know for certain is that some highly respected pros use the term. Still, you can call it a bolo if you prefer, thus demonstrating your extensive knowledge of tennis jargon. These things always make an impression.

A reverse forehand is actually the opposite of a squash shot; still on the run, however, it is hit by swinging up and toward the side fence instead of down. The racquet follow-through is distinctive. The racquet goes flying back behind your head like a stealth bomber.

Windshield wiper

The 'windshield wiper' forehand should very definitely be part of the tennis bluffer's armoury. Just to complicate things further, this shot is a form of topspin. Instead of making topspin conventionally, with the racquet head aimed toward your target on the other side of the court, your racquet moves in the motion of a windshield wiper: up, over and down in front of your body like an upside-down U (or a lower-case N, if you must). Frequently, the hitter's arm finishes around the waist. It not only gives topspin, but sidespin as well. That's two shots for the price of one.

The windshield wiper (WW) mostly uses what some pros call the 'double-bend' forehand. The WW entails hitting the ball with a bent elbow and a bent wrist. It looks as ugly as lipstick on a pig, but if you can make bacon from it…

This stroke type can be difficult to identify because there are as many swing paths between a normal topspin and a windshield wiper as there are flavours of ice cream.

Run-around

Finally, there is the run-around. As mentioned earlier, forehands are just about every player's favourite shot. Tennis players will do almost anything to hit a good one, including buying tickets to the tennis club's charity ball.

Frequently, when an opponent hits a weakish ball to the backhand side, players will dash over to the backhand side of the court so they can use their confident and penetrating forehands instead of their puny puff-pastry backhands. If someone asks if you run around your backhand, reply 'yes'; why wouldn't you want to attack with your strongest shot?

FOREHAND STANCES

Most people take stances, unless they're politicians, who would sooner donate a kidney than take a stance. Forehands, unlike politicians, do take a stance – in fact, multiple stances. Through the decades since Harry and Juan knocked a ball to and fro in Birmingham, tennis players have devised an assortment of ways to stand up while hitting a forehand.

Closed stance

The closed stance entails the non-dominant leg stepping across and in front of the dominant leg in order to hit the ball. This stance is considered 'old style' and is therefore to be shunned when expressing a) your opinion of the best stance and b) the stance you personally execute.

Rod Laver (*see* page 79) used this stance back in the 1960s. What on earth was he thinking?

Neutral stance

In the neutral stance, the non-dominant leg steps directly in front of the dominant leg. All you need to know if the subject comes up is that the two feet are perpendicular to the net when hitting the ball. You can claim this is the best stance 'under certain circumstances'. Just don't speculate on what they might be.

Open stance

The open stance is the newest and, therefore, the most acceptable. It is said to generate more power, using the relatively new and improved 'angular' momentum, than the old-style 'linear' momentum ever did. This is a useful observation for dropping idly into conversation, even if you haven't got the faintest idea what it means.

The open stance means the player is facing the net and only turns his or her shoulders perpendicular to the net. So, after hitting a forehand, players are automatically left handily in the ready position. That fact alone is really all you need to know to declare this stance as the preferred one. The ready position is the one a player uses while waiting for the opponent to hit his or her next shot, and entails facing the opponent with feet more than shoulder-width apart and both hands on the racquet.

Don't forget Always claim the forehand to be your favourite/best shot. That's because it's much more effective than the backhand.

BACKHANDS

Backhands are not fabulous. There's a reason why every player with a forehand runs around their backhand like it's Typhoid Mary. And players will continue to do this no matter how good their backhands become. Why? Because forehands, you will emphasise, are always the better shot choice.

There are some exceptions to this rule, as ever, and if you were to scour the tennis clubs of every country in the United Nations, you would uncover some players who possess the backhand-dominant gene. These people are rarer than teetotallers at a stag party.

The message here is: never claim your backhand as your best or favourite shot. You would be telegraphing to everyone within earshot that your tennis is about as normal as a supermodel's diet regime.

Players who possess the backhand-dominant gene are rarer than teetotallers at a stag party.

One-handed backhands are becoming rarer every day; only purists use them. The reason people hit backhands with two hands is that it makes it a more secure shot. It's pretty much a forehand with the non-dominant arm but with the dominant hand on board for stability's sake. On the whole it works; most players today use the two-hander.

Two-handed backhands are not all rainbows and unicorns, though. You should point out that since players hold on with both hands, their reach is compromised. Also, hitting balls low to the ground is a more difficult task with two hands than it is with one.

Topspin or flat shots are all the two-handers can muster. If you feel the need to slice a shot, just take the non-dominant hand off the grip. Then, of course, you temporarily become a one-hand backhander.

Two-handers hold the racquet by its grip with the dominant hand and by its throat with the other. Then they slide their weaker hand down on top of their dominant hand to hit a backhand. When most players see the ball coming to their backhand, their first thought will be: 'Can I run around it?' Just as quickly they'll more than likely decide: 'No! Dammit!' They'll then turn their shoulders to face the side fence, take the racquet back with both hands, step across themselves and swing the racquet forward. With luck, the strung part will make clean contact with the ball which will zing unerringly into a part of the court their opponent wasn't expecting. But more frequently it will zing unerringly into the net.

BASIC BACKHANDS

Topspin

Yes, topspins are possible with a backhand using one or two hands. The mechanics are the same as with the forehand. However, they're not as powerful or accurate as a forehand. None of your backhands are. Unless you're a world-class athlete, you're almost sure to look like a bumbling cretin when hitting one.

Slice

One-handed backhand slice shots can be very effective. Slices are very graceful-looking and are used to keep the ball low. When the ball is low, your opponent must hit it back up and over the net. Hitting up makes it very difficult for your opponent to hit a winner.

BACKHAND STANCES

Closed stance
The backhand version of the closed stance is similar to the forehand version but uses the other (dominant) leg to cross over. Closed stances can be used for both one- and two-handed backhands. The majority of players use the closed stance while hitting backhands.

Neutral stance
The neutral stance can be used with backhands, but it is not advised.

Open stance
The open-stance backhand is rarer than a politician with a conscience. Indeed, for many years this stance was considered only possible in theory. However, it seems that Serena Williams didn't get the memo, because she routinely uses an open-stance backhand and hits a remarkable number of winners.

YOUR COOL SHOTS

VOLLEYS

Volleys will be an indispensable part of your game. When you claim to be able to volley, it means you have been playing tennis for a while and that you even know extra tennis skills like how to pick up a tennis ball without using your hands. (Incidentally, this is a useful device for bluffing. It involves bringing the racquet head down on a stationary ball and using the resultant bounce to bring it under control. All pros do it, so practise it as much as possible. It's not that hard, although it looks very stupid when it goes wrong.)

Volleys are hit straight out of the air. No bounces. Tennis wimps stay behind the baseline and let the oncoming ball bounce first. Letting the ball bounce allows the court to remove a good measure of the incoming ball's speed. That's why so many players opt to stand as far behind the baseline as they can manage. This irritates the hell out of volleyers.

In virtually every case, a volley is hit from inside

the service box (the part of the court where the serve is supposed to land). That's because that is where the player is standing. Players stand there on purpose – precisely so they can volley.

You see, volleys are, by their very nature, offensive shots that aggressive players use a lot – in between fist-pumping and loud exhortations of 'Just f***ing COME ON!' (And that's one of the more printable ones.)

Nowadays, volleys are most often found in doubles games, but there are two volley scenarios in a game of singles. One goes like this: during a backcourt rally, player A hits a shot that lands short on the other side of the net. Player B runs forward and hits his or her next shot into one of player A's corners. Player B then sets up position about six feet from the net to await A's weak return. When it comes, player B volleys the ball into A's other corner for a winner.

The other scenario is this: player A hits a serve so hard and so well placed that player B's return is a wounded duck of a floater. Anticipating this feeble attempt at a return, player A follows his or her serve to the net to volley it away with disdain.

The truth is, both of those scenarios were played out regularly in the not-too-distant past. Back then, the courts were faster and the racquets and strings were made differently. Today's scenario (there is only one) is different: you blast Mach 1 groundstrokes at each other until one player develops a cramp in one of the major muscle groups. Additionally, although today's racquets are now engineered to produce hugely powerful shots capable of punching holes in Kevlar body armour, the new strings are engineered to spin balls like an aeroplane propeller. Spin, as you will now know, provides the sort of control required to keep the ball from being launched over the fence and into the next postcode.

Still, it takes a conspicuous amount of courage to come into the net to volley because there's an excellent chance that a tennis ball will find its way on an unerring trajectory into some really sensitive part of your anatomy at a dangerous speed. Even from the backcourt.

To volley, you just wave your racquet head at the incoming woolly missile before it bounces, then see what happens. Once you're able to do that, you can incorporate some racquet movement; forward tends to help.

LOBS

Lobs are defined as shots that are hit softly and high. They are used to hit the ball over the head of any opponent deranged enough to be standing close to the net. They are also quite useful for buying time.

Lobs were devised by mercilessly bullied players who were being pushed around on the court by high-protein-devouring brutes. To slow them and their muscular strokeplay down, the persecuted little guys concocted the lob. The brutes crush the lob back, only to be lobbed again. And then again. And again. Eventually, they become so frustrated that they attack the net post with their racquets until there's nothing left but a graphite pulp.

OVERHEAD (SLAM)

Overheads are sensational. These types of shots are powerful explosions of guided terminal velocity with well-deserved reputations as dramatic point-enders. They're great to watch, that is, if you're watching pro tennis on TV. They're also great to watch at your local club, especially if you like a good laugh as a hacker slices the ball off the frame of the racquet and into his mouth.

All good pros have to have dynamite overheads or else they'd be bartenders. They laugh in the face of lobs. 'Bwahaha,' they guffaw as they slam overheads into the corners with a sneer.

It's about as easy to execute a good half-volley as it is to share a bath with a frightened skunk.

Overheads are hit like serves, but instead of the usual interminable set-up until everything is absolutely in sync, the player is required to hit a high ball that effectively falls out of the sky. With perfect timing and coordination the slammer then crushes the ball like an empty beer can for a dramatic winner. Boys and girls swoon.

HALF-VOLLEY

First off, half-volleys are not volleys. Indeed, the player has to let the ball bounce first. (Even though he or she would rather not.)

So, just like a normal shot then? Almost, but not quite. What differentiates the half-volley is that the ball is struck just after it ricochets off the court right in front of the player aiming to hit it back. Here's the crucial bit: the ball has not actually reached the apex of its bounce – in other words, it is still rising when it's hit. Unsurprisingly, the shot is also known as an 'on-the-rise' shot. Bluffers should be aware that it's about as easy to execute a good half-volley as it is to share a bath with a frightened skunk.

LOB VOLLEY

These tricky little devils are volleys that players hit from inside the service box, over the head and beyond the reach of their opponent who will also be standing in the service box. The danger is obvious: if hit too short, the opponent will attempt to convert it into a thundering overhead straight into that private place where the sun don't shine. Even if the attempt misses its target, it might well hit another which could be equally painful.

DROP SHOT

Drop shots are shots that drop just over the net. Players hit them there to annoy their opponents. What makes drop shots great is that they are so satisfying when they come off. A player approaches the shot as if it were going to be hit with maximum prejudice (in other words, out). The opponent backs off the baseline, index finger already poised in the 'out' position. Then the drop shot comes out of nowhere.

The opponent is so stunned at this unexpected display of a quasi strategy that he/she staggers for a second, then races to the ball and lunges for it as if it were a falling Ming vase. Even if they do get to lay their racquet on the ball, the chances are that it will simply be spooned into the net. Or, the evilly cackling drop-shotter will be right there to smash the return between the opponent's legs in a bold stroke of pure intimidation. Note that the American player Bobby Riggs, big in the 1940s, was considered to have had the greatest drop shot of all time – off both his forehand and backhand.

TWEENER

This is a shot hit in the backcourt by a player whose back is facing the net, between the legs. It is a do-or-die shot – a last resort for keeping the ball in play. Indeed, it's the agony or the ecstasy shot. (It's more likely to be the agony.)

GRIPS

There are as many ways to hold a tennis racquet as there are positions in the Kama Sutra – although they're not nearly as much fun, or so one is led to believe. While they are largely overlooked, grips are the foundation of all tennis strokes. The precise manner in which you hold the racquet has a major impact on each ball you hit, in much the same way your grip on a club does in golf. So you should know about the following:

Eastern

This grip is used throughout the world. It can be compared to 'shaking hands' with the handle when the strings of the racquet head are perpendicular to the court. It is generally considered to be as 'old style' as big-band music and long tennis flannels. Though many players use it to this day, more do not. Those who use it do so primarily for groundstrokes (i.e., forehands and backhands) at waist level or lower.

Continental

Sometimes called the 'hammer' grip, this is used by players for shots other than groundstrokes: the serve, volley and overhead. It's the one grip that could be used for every shot, but having just the one way of holding the handle isn't advised.

Western

There are a great many variations of the western grip, but the most basic is similar to shaking hands with a racquet whose strings are pointed face down. This grip works well for forehands that are hit at elbow height or higher – in other words, high-bouncing balls.

This grip is said to have been devised in those countries that favour high-bouncing hard courts. A side effect of this court type is the two-handed backhand. Why? Well, the alternative – hitting a high one-handed backhand – is as easy as slicing bread with a spanner.

Hawaiian

The Hawaiian is the most extreme of the western grips. It entails cupping the handle from underneath, as if holding your hand out for a handout. It is known for causing arm and wrist problems if employed incorrectly and is thus a godsend to bluffers who can blame it for all sorts of defects. ('I was trying out an extreme version of the extreme Hawaiian and something just went "ping". Never been the same since.')

Every good bluffer should claim to have a weapon, even if they don't know what it is.

ANYONE FOR TENNIS?

Sooner or later you might find yourself actually having to step out onto a tennis court to put your bluffing skills to the test. There are two main forms of the competitive game. There could be a third if you count playing against a brick wall, but people tend not to – unless they really are short of friends.

SINGLES

Singles tennis involves two players going head to head, toe to toe, nose to nose, lip to… No, forget that last one.

Singles players are in it for the glory and, if they're pros, for the money too. To that end, successful singles players must train hard like boxers, hit thousands and thousands of tennis balls, eat right, and sleep on orthopaedic mattresses – mainly alone – to ensure restful sleep. If you claim to be a singles player, base it on your independent 'mindset'. Tell others you want to beat your opponents into roadkill. Tell them you only play doubles when you must, such as when your boss orders it as a team-building exercise.

Most singles players don't play doubles because:

* they don't get to hit enough balls;
* they don't like sharing; and
* they can't play doubles.

A doubles match allows lower-level players who are well versed in doubles play to beat more highly skilled singles players who don't know how to play doubles. This differential, coupled with the unfamiliar experience of losing to less-skilled players, infuriates the technically superior, but doubles-ignorant, singles players. Typically, they'd rather not engage in doubles play at all, because they end up running around aimlessly like mice in a maze.

Singles and doubles skills are not mutually exclusive, however. You should know that there are those who can play both effectively. So drop into conversation at an appropriate moment that multiple singles Grand Slam winner, John 'Superbrat' McEnroe, is also considered to be, perhaps, the best doubles player ever. Martina Navratilova was pretty good as well. It's just that most players are more adept at one or the other. You should boast to people that you play both ways. It only takes twice the knowledge and, to be honest, it doesn't require much.

There are styles of singles play which the bluffer must claim to prefer, based mainly on what you consider to be your strong point (or points). They are exemplified by the following player types:

SERVE-AND-VOLLEYER

The serve-and-volley style means that you have a big and powerful serve – one that people have a difficult time returning. Even if they do return the ball, they tend to float it back with all the penetrating power of a soap bubble. To take advantage of these puny returns, you follow your serve to the net where you can volley it unmercifully into the open court.

Serve-and-volleyers don't like to get into long rallies where they get yanked from one side of the court to the other. They hate that. They're at their best when moving forward and back with metronomic precision.

If you still want to claim this style as your own, you can tell others that you modelled it after Sampras or Navratilova. Unless you're as observant as, say, a fruit bat, you will have noticed that they have both retired. No current pro plays this way because the courts have been slowed down so much that the balls pop up and wave a friendly hello.

ALL-COURTER

The all-court style means you have a good all-round game. You may even have a weapon. Every good tennis bluffer should claim to have a weapon, even if they don't know what it is.

In tennis lingo it means 'a reliable shot that can put your opponent in a defensive position'. Closing your eyes and hoping for the best is sometimes quite a useful weapon as well. All-courters used to follow their powerful first serves and hard penetrating shots to the net, and they tended to have one-handed backhands. But, yet again, the slower courts have taken their toll, making this type of player a dying breed. In fact, if you claim this style, claim you modelled your game on Roger Federer on a fast court. (The Belgian player Justine Henin, probably the last female player of this type retired in 2008, at 25, when she was still ranked number one in the world.) 'I don't know why we're not talking about Justine Henin all the time because, for her size, she's the greatest athlete we've ever seen,' said Billie Jean King, who knows a thing or two about these things.

AGGRESSIVE BASELINER

This style of player likes to bash groundstrokes from behind the baseline, which forces their opponents into weaker and weaker positions until they ultimately hit the ball out, or hit a short ball (one that can be hit from on or inside the baseline) which invites the sort of compassion a medium-rare rib-eye might expect from a hungry pit bull.

No one is more aggressive from the baseline than Roger Federer.

These players have very good foot speed and are in good physical condition. They also usually have two-handed backhands. Note the word 'usually' because no one is more aggressive from the baseline than Roger Federer. (He has a one-handed backhand, if you're keeping track.)

Serena Williams and Maria Sharapova are good female examples. But, to be honest, the vast majority of players on the women's tour are aggressive baseliners.

COUNTERPUNCHER

Counterpunchers have gifted foot speed and are notoriously defensive-minded. They tend to wait, happy to be in a metronomic rally until their frustrated opponent either falls asleep or tries forcing a low-percentage shot to make something – anything – happen. It is then that the counterpuncher fires off a high-reward, missile-like winner down the line or an extreme cross-court-angled winner.

DOUBLES

Doubles is tennis's idea of a team game.

There are three main versions: mixed doubles, where a man and a woman play another man and a woman; men's doubles (sometimes 'gentlemen's' doubles), where two men play two other men; and women's doubles (sometimes 'ladies' doubles), when two women play two other women. There might well be other sorts of doubles involving sexual, religious, ethnic, adaptive, professional or vocational criteria, but they don't tend to feature in major tournaments (yet).

The principal aim in all types of tennis is the same: to

beat the opposition. This can lead to all sorts of tension (on both sides of the net).

Doubles, like poker, can be played in more than one way. The officially recognised doubles styles are as follows:

BOTH UP

Good players employ the 'both up' style of doubles. This means pretty much what it says, in the sense that both players tend to play 'at the net'. Net players are unusually fearless and don't mind charging forward to intimidate overhead slammers. The both up style is preferred by the vast majority of Grand Slam doubles teams. It's effective but it has its disadvantages, namely running back to the baseline to retrieve perfectly placed lobs hit by the annoying doubles players who adopt certain other styles. Such as:

BOTH BACK

Slower, more methodical players mainly prefer the 'both back' style of doubles. 'Back' means 'at the baseline'. There, players are safer from those stinging balls that good, powerful players deliberately aim at their opponents to intimidate them.

Proponents of this style need to communicate efficiently because doubles, by definition, requires teamwork. Each partner must know what the other is doing. And, if they don't, they'll need to direct each other's movement. That involves a fair bit of yelling at each other.

You won't hear any yelling when watching doubles on TV, especially when 'both backers' are playing, mainly because they don't televise doubles. Well, maybe during a singles rain delay, or when some poor schmuck loses 6-0, 6-0 in 55 minutes. On the rare occasions you do see a televised doubles match, there'll be very little spoken communication because the players will probably know what they're doing.

But down at your local courts or club, doubles players will issue a litany of seemingly random words, trying to impart to their partners valuable positioning information. Here are some of the words you might hear (and what they really mean):

Yours ('I'm not touching that mother.')
Mine ('I'll take that little sucker.')
Switch ('I'd be more comfortable playing over there.')
Back ('Watch out! I screwed up my lob.')
Up ('What the hell are you doing back there?')

Both backers almost never win on talent. Their standard operating procedure (SOP) is to bore the opposition to death.

UP AND BACK

The 'up and back' style is used by teams consisting of one net player and one backcourt player. It would seem to be the sensible compromise. The player at the net is up there in a poaching role to intercept their opponents' return for a put-away. If that technique fails, their partner is still in position at the baseline to return the ball, thus giving the net partner another crack at hitting a glorious winner.

Actually, the up and back style is only useful against an incompetent both back team. A competent both back team can lob them to their hearts' content.

The up and back style is entirely useless against a both up team. Not only can the both uppers take advantage of the huge put-away alley that exists between the up partner and the back partner, but also, the sole player at the net becomes an enticing target the size of Stonehenge.

GAMESMANSHIP AND EXCUSES

In any analysis of unsportsmanlike behaviour, bluffers should never use the word 'cheating'. Gamesmanship, on the other hand, is a permissible tactic – simply because it is allowed by the rules (however deplorable it might be). It is sometimes also known as 'getting inside an opponent's head', or what used to be called 'putting off'. Mess with someone's mind, and you mess with their game. There are many ways of doing this.

You might have noticed that when tournament matches get uncomfortably close, some pros tend to start distracting their opponents from playing well by pushing the boundaries of the International Tennis Federation (ITF) rules. Some players routinely violate time limits. Others (there are countless examples) take legal medical timeouts only when the going gets tough and an 'in the zone' opponent needs cooling off. Still others have been known to get illegal coaching from their friends' box.

Grunting, shrieking, swearing, screaming, racquet throwing, and abusing the official are all additional ways of putting an opponent off in a pro match.

Ball bouncing before serving is a time-honoured method of slowing the game, and cooling down a fired-up opponent. There are no firm rules on the number of ball bounces permissible while setting up. Novak Djokovic was known for bouncing until his opponent became catatonic with boredom. He was once observed performing a 29-time ball bounce, but the umpire failed to intervene (on the grounds that he was probably dozing). Grunting, shrieking, swearing, screaming, racquet throwing, and abusing the official are all additional ways of putting an opponent off in a pro match. Sometimes it's worth a penalty to disturb the composure of a player on a hot streak.

AMATEUR GAMESMANSHIP

Of course, the vast majority of tennis matches are between amateur players who don't get to rely on official enforcers monitoring their transgressions. By necessity, they play matches according to the 'honour' system. The players make their own rules about drink breaks, cramp relief, knee strapping, blister wrapping, religious observance, and line calls. The inevitable disputes regarding the latter are generally brought to a satisfactory conclusion for both players by negotiation. Not infrequently, this negotiation involves a convincing headbutt.

Gamesmanship resembles an infomercial. It is disturbingly common and designed to separate you from your senses. When playing an expert gamesmanshipper, the desire to win stems from knowing that, should you lose, your nemesis is going to perform a celebratory dance so elaborate that it might well qualify for the 'All-time-10-most-watched list' on YouTube.

There are degrees of gamesmanship. It can be as subtle as a baby's breath, or as obvious as a neon sign flashing 'unsportsmanlike behaviour'.

To gamesmanshippers, playing the 'game' can be more rewarding than playing tennis. To them, the ability to totally distract you with underhand ploys and schemes to the point where you leap over the net with your racquet raised in a fit of bloodthirsty rage, ready to accept a forfeit and certain jail time, is vitally important. They like to win that way. In fact, they prefer to win that way, because they're essentially sociopaths.

Some common forms of amateur gamesmanship include:

1. slowing the match down to the speed of coastal erosion by adopting tactics such as replacing shoelaces on an opponent's game or set point;
2. trying to speed up the match via quick serves (serving when an opponent is retrieving balls, nose-blowing, adjusting a contact lens, etc.);

3. giving the balls back to the server by making them take long trips back to the fence or with point-blank overheads;
4. questioning an opponent's line calls during the warm-up;
5. offering wholly insincere sentiments of sympathy when an opponent makes a mistake (e.g., 'Hard cheese!' as exemplified by the actor Terry-Thomas in the definitive tennis gamesmanship scene from the film *School for Scoundrels*); or
6. displaying a rifle stock from a tennis bag.

Always claim to empathise with those who decry the practice of gamesmanship. It is an insidious virus that threatens the very foundations of the game, you will say as you simultaneously try to figure out where their vulnerability lies. If, for example, you hear: 'If there's one thing I can't stand, it's a six-bounce server,' then you know what you have to do.

MAKING EXCUSES

Since at any given time, 50% of players lose their matches, players are prone to assigning blame for their losses in order to save face with their peers. To establish 'blame' as a respectable 'cause' and not an 'excuse', you must explain that there were 'extenuating circumstances'.

Tennis is fraught with extenuating circumstances. People lose for a number of reasons (which are nearly always in the mind):

* **The player that beat them was about 10 levels better.** It's okay to lose to a really good player. For example, you could tell others that you lost to Andy Murray 6-1, 6-0. Subsequently, people would assume you were a highly capable player. After all, you got a game off Sir Andy! Legions of fellow players would sit at your feet in reverential awe as you recounted how you called his service out eight times in a row.

  People don't mind losing to players who are clearly superior. In fact, they're proud to announce they even played them. Moreover, if you related that an Olympic champion then bought you a post-match beer and offered to pay for an eye test, you would find yourself with a bunch of new friends.

* **They were cheated out of the match.** And, it may be true. After all, since there are no official enforcers, cheaters feel free to operate brazenly out in the open. You will never stoop to their level – by deliberately calling a ball out when you know it was in. Perish the thought. A stolen victory is a hollow one. And bluffers should not stoop to that level. Not at all.

* **They weren't playing at their outstanding best.** Their reasons will vary. Some will claim the sun was in their eyes. Or they'd been stung by a flying insect. Or, they had to play with a backup racquet with broken strings. Or their socks didn't match.

More often, these losers will claim a mysterious ailment which comes under the general heading of 'Acute

Hyperbolic Paralogism'. Some will even offer the well-worn excuse 'tennis elbow'. You can offer it too. Just grab your arm below your elbow and wince. Then, gritting your teeth, mention how your doctor told you it was the worst case he'd ever seen and that it must be rested at all costs. 'My problem is that I've never been the type to do what the doctor ordered,' you will say – hinting at your extraordinary reserves of doggedness and reckless fortitude.

Tennis elbow flare-up is the most popular of the standard excuses for the sort of incompetence evidenced by club and amateur players. You should invoke this excuse yourself by taking every opportunity to wrap whole rolls of Velcro strapping around your forearms as proof of your infirmity.

Excuseology is an up-and-coming science in sports. Borrow freely from the following list of crank excuses and their meanings that only a real tennis bluffer would recognise and appreciate.

Tennis elbow An extremely sensitive and painful elbow condition brought on by hitting the ball every which way but correctly. The *ne plus ultra* of a bluffer's supposed tennis injuries.

Cheater's eye A black-and-blue discoloration around the eye, usually in the shape of a fist.

Netman's neck A ricked neck caused by watching an excessive number of lobs fly overhead and out of reach.

Server's shin A compound fracture of the shin caused by smashing it with the racquet while serving with too much enthusiasm.

Hacker's knee Sclerotic knee joints caused by a lack of bending, flexing, stretching, or anything else involving movement.

Faulter's foot Painful fallen arches belonging to an irate doubles player, caused by stamping in protest over a partner's constant foot-faulting.

Bragger's lip A swollen, sometimes bloodied lip, caused by excessive bragging about a victory over an irritable opponent.

Pumper's forearm A sprained forearm due to excessive fist-pumping up-and-down after winning a point.

Showman's groin A deep, excruciating pain in the groin, typically caused by violent contact with the ball or racquet while attempting a between-the-legs trick shot.

Liner's finger A severely dislocated finger, contracted by constantly pointing 'out' at every ball that lands within a ball's width of the line and having it bent by a disputatious opponent.

Racquet wrist A painful condition of the wrist caused by excessive attempts to launch a racquet into the stratosphere after a disputed line call.

Slapper's hip A deep, painful contusion on the hip caused by constant exhortations to do better.

CHOKING AND ZONING

No analysis of the power of the mind to affect the result of a tennis match could be complete without consideration of the terrible affliction known as 'choking' – a state of mind defined as 'the complete loss of basic motor skills, sometimes even bodily functions, and/or elementary reasoning powers while pre-experiencing a post-match, humiliating loss'.

A useful bluffing note is that this condition is recognised and well-documented. In other sports it is known as the 'yips', but its official name is 'focal dystonia' – a neurological condition that affects a muscle or group of muscles in a specific part of the body causing involuntary muscular contractions and abnormal postures. So if you find yourself lying in a foetal position in the middle of the court, moaning softly, and feebly waving your racquet at a hail of imaginary balls, you might as well accept the fact that you've choked.

Choking is the opposite of playing in the zone. Playing 'in the zone' means 'you temporarily play at a level far greater than your skill'. Whereas most players choke on a weekly, sometimes daily, basis, 'zoning' occurs about as often as politicians tell the truth. The best-known symptom of zoning is that everything you do turns out amazingly right. All net-cord shots land on the other side of the net. If you lob short, a freak gust of wind pushes it deep. If you fall down, your opponent twists an ankle. Zoning is amazing. Sadly, it is not something the bluffer will experience often (if at all), except in the telling.

Tennis followers have long known that choking occurs at various stages of a match according to each player's individual choke threshold. Some players only choke during crucial, match-teetering points, like tiebreakers. Other players start choking on important points, such as break points. Then, there are those who choke whenever the balls come out of the can.

The most terrible example of a choke is a second serve that bounces on the server's side – of his or her own service line. When that happens you might just as well pack up and go home, not forgetting to throw your racquet into a cement mixer on the way.

John McEnroe had a tempestuous relationship with everyone and everything, including his shoes.

HALL OF FAME

At some point in your tennis bluffing career, you will be required to venture an opinion on who's who in the pantheon of great players. This brief list, which does not claim to be comprehensive or in any particular order (like every other list in this book), also includes some of the most prominent current players. So you might recognise a name or two and feel better about your bluffing credentials already.

THE GENTLEMEN

Fred Perry

He was English and won a few major tournaments, like Wimbledon, in the days when men wore spotless white flannels while playing. These trousers had pockets but they weren't really necessary because he won just £10 for his Wimbledon victory in 1936. Perry is best known for being the last Brit to have won a Grand Slam tournament before Andy Murray. That was an unusually barren period of 76 years (even by British sporting standards). He was also well known (and envied) for being a bit of a ladies' man, enjoying affairs with Hollywood stars Jean Harlow, Loretta Young and Marlene Dietrich, among others. When he had time he spent it refining the world's first sweatband, later supplemented by his own sports clothing brand.

Bill Tilden

Tilden was American and, by all accounts, tall. Back in the 1920s, 'Big Bill' dominated men's tennis. He was gay – as the world eventually found out after a couple of arrests on morals charges and his subsequent imprisonment. In those days, rather like playing for prize money, being gay was just not done.

Don Budge

Budge was also an American and for five years in the 1930s and early 1940s he was the world number one, both as amateur and professional. The tall, gawky son of a Scottish footballer who had emigrated to the US, he won the singles, doubles and mixed doubles at Wimbledon in 1937 and '38. He turned pro in 1939 which somewhat curtailed his involvement in Grand Slam competitions. By then he had become world famous as the first player, of either sex, to win a Grand Slam (see page 95 – 'Major Majors'). Aged 23 he was the youngest ever tennis player to have achieved this, something which looks unlikely to be eclipsed in the modern era. At some time during an up and down career he triumphed over most of the best known players of his era including Fred Perry, Bill Tilden, Bunny Austin, Bobby Riggs, and – at the age of 39 – he beat the best player in the world, Pancho Gonzales.

Pancho Gonzales

A Mexican-American, big from the late 1940s to 1960s, he had a huge serve-and-volley game. In 1969 Gonzales was famous for his part in what was then the longest game ever played at Wimbledon. As a 41-year-old, he met Charlie Pasarell, a Puerto Rican 16 years his junior. The game finished 22-24, 1-6, 16-14, 6-3, 11-9 with Gonzales the eventual winner. There were no tiebreaks in those days.

Rod Laver

Known as the 'Rocket', Laver was an Aussie and arguably the best player ever (even better than Federer). You can argue the point because he won two calendar Grand Slams. A Grand Slam consists of winning the Australian Open, the French Open, Wimbledon and the US Open all in one calendar year.* (It was a big deal back in the 1960s. It might still be. However, since no man has done it since Laver, we really don't know.) For the record, Laver was left-handed. And freckly. At the last count, Laver still holds the record for the most singles titles won in the history of tennis, with 200 career titles (although many were as an amateur).

*While this is the original definition of 'Grand Slam', the term is now frequently used in a broader context. So, for clarity, it's best to call it a 'calendar Grand Slam' when referring to a player's winning all four titles in a calendar year, and 'career Grand Slam' when the player has won all four over the course of his or her career. The former is the greater achievement (*See* also 'Major Majors', page 95).

Arthur Ashe

The first black player to win a major singles title. He has a stadium named after him at Flushing Meadows, home of the US Open. Ashe is well known for not playing the 1972 South African Open – mainly because they wouldn't let him in the country.

Jimmy Connors

An American lefty, multiple majors title holder (eight) and former world number one, Connors was an extremely competitive player. He won 109 pro singles titles in his career – that's more than any other male tennis player. His story is replete with interesting bluffing points. He was Maria Sharapova's coach, until she sacked him after just one match in 2013. In 1974 he won every major tournament except the French Open, in which he didn't compete. At one time, he was engaged to fellow American player Chris Evert (the tennis world was enchanted, but their relationship wasn't). He was infamous for single-handedly stopping Bjorn Borg from winning a US Open title. He dated Miss World, and ultimately married a former Playboy model. Where did it all go wrong for 'Jimbo'?

Bjorn Borg

A Swede, possibly the first genuine teen pin-up in tennis in the 1970s, known for winning from the backcourt. He owned a two-handed backhand and a headband, and was known as the 'IceBorg' because he was extraordinarily, even weirdly, cool under pressure. He was doubly strange because he won on both clay and grass surfaces with equal efficacy. He never won the Australian or US Opens.

John McEnroe

An Irish-American lefty, best known for his eloquent on-court outbursts directed at umpires, such as, 'You *cannot* be serious!', 'You guys are the absolute pits of the world!', and 'Answer my question...the QUESTION, JERK!' When he wasn't abusing officials, he was abusing his racquet (which isn't quite as unnatural as it sounds). His retirement from the pro-tennis circuit in 1992 came as a blow to the world's TV networks. McEnroe was christened 'Superbrat' by the British tabloid press. He was, and remains, the only Wimbledon champion not to be given honorary membership of the club (although he was accorded the honour after a subsequent victory).

Ivan Lendl

A Czech who defected to the USA when it was popular for Czechs to do so. He won eight major titles and is best known for his merciless, take-no-prisoners manner on the court. After retiring from tennis, he took up golf. Unlike tennis, he plays golf left-handed. He also coached Andy Murray.

Stefan Edberg

A Swedish player, big in the 1980s and early 1990s, who was every bit as cool a competitor as his fellow countryman, Borg (and arguably better looking). An old-style serve-and-volleyer, he won six Grand Slam titles. Best known for being such a good sport that they named the ATP's men's Sportsmanship Award after him.

Pete Sampras

A noticeably hirsute Spartan-American (really), known for winning a whole lot of Wimbledon titles – he won 14 Grand Slam titles in total – by serving and volleying. Something of a mild-mannered gentleman on court, and therefore much less interesting than his compatriots 'Johnny Mac' and 'Jimbo'. 'Pistol Pete's' mother emigrated from Sparta, Greece, and his father was born in the USA to a Greek father and a Jewish mother. For a while he was unbeatable.

Andre Agassi

An Iranian-American (or it might be Assyrian) with several major titles. Another pin-up, he was so loved by the media that he did advertising spots for non-tennis products (another major accomplishment). Although he was once married to actress Brooke Shields, who had even bigger eyebrows than Sampras, he is now married to German-built, also-retired player Steffi Graf (*see* page 87), who had (and probably still has) the best legs in tennis history.

Roger Federer

A Swiss player with the most career Grand Slam titles, the most Grand Slam finals, semi-finals, quarter-finals, victories, and a bunch of other records. 'Fed' has won nine Stefan Edberg Sportsmanship Awards and speaks four languages fluently. His strokes are so elegant and his movements so graceful that he is said to move like a dancer around the court. He is strangely attractive to women of a certain age (mostly of the more mature vintage). Celebrities also love him and are often seen in his player's box (courtside seats for friends and family). Arguably the best player ever. Or is that Laver? Discuss. Federer engaged the previously noted tennis sportsmanship exponent, Stefan Edberg, as his coach between 2013 and 2015. Together, they were so nice and so polite, you might be forgiven for thinking that they lacked the killer instinct (don't be fooled).

Rafael Nadal

A lefty Spaniard from the island of Mallorca, 'Rafa' is the best clay-courter – ever. No argument. In fact, he has won 11 French (clay) Opens. They should probably name a stadium after him at Roland Garros – or at the very least a water fountain. He has also won three US Opens, two Wimbledon titles, and one Australian Open. Irresistibly attractive to women of a certain age – any age. Nadal's coach is his uncle, Toni Nadal ('Uncle Toni'). He has admitted that his uncle's training regime was so tough when he was a boy that he used to go home in tears, with the words 'mummy's boy' ringing in his ears. Earn extra bluffing points for saying that it was probably something more like 'niño de mamá'!

Novak Djokovic

Another number-one male player in recent years, Djokovic is Serbian and notoriously gluten-free and body aware. Bizarrely he once employed infamous German lothario and former multiple Grand Slam winner, Boris Becker, as his coach. Becker, a cigar-chomping, wine-quaffing *bon viveur*, is not the most obvious advertisement for healthy living, but he does have a keen competitive edge, having won a few major titles of his own. Meanwhile, 'The Serbinator' is well known for his habit of sitting in a pressurised CVAC chamber known as a 'Space Egg' that mimics altitude changes and which he believes boosts performance.

Andy Murray

A Scot, he has a mound named after him at Wimbledon and is a knight of the round table (or something). Notoriously taciturn, monotonic, and unusually tearful on occasions, he was the first male Brit* to win a major tournament (the 2012 US Open) since Fred Perry. In the same year he won the first of two Olympic Gold medals, and followed that with the 2013 Wimbledon title after taking on a new coach, multiple-major-winner Ivan Lendl. The doleful Czech instructed Murray to play more aggressively, and so he did. He became noticeably more aggressive and roared like a lion every time he won a point. Sadly he became something of a wounded lion, beset by persistent injuries after adding a second Wimbledon title to his list of Grand Slam victories in 2016. Thereafter his competitiveness was hampered by a serious hip problem which required a possibly career-ending operation in early 2019. A grateful nation prays for a Lazarus-like recovery.

* There is a long-held suspicion that the UK (English) media have derided Sir Andy as 'Scottish when he loses, British when he wins'. A 2015 study by Stirling University of press reports between 2005 and 2014 proved that this was categorically not the case. The suspicion lingers nonetheless.

The Bryan Brothers

Bob and Mike Bryan are American identical twins, and unarguably the best doubles team ever. They have won every major doubles tournament, Olympic gold in London 2012, and a career Grand Slam. They are so good at doubles that they don't have to play singles to make a living. Which is why you have never heard of them, and why they are on this bluffer's list.

THE LADIES

Suzanne Lenglen

A female player who dominated women's tennis from 1914 to 1926 (around the time when women were expected to be fully clothed on court), she was six times Wimbledon champion in both singles and doubles. She's useful bluffer fodder, as in: 'best/worst since Suzanne Lenglen'. It doesn't matter that it is unlikely that anyone living today has ever seen her play, or is likely to have heard of her. She became a media sensation when she introduced bare arms and ankles at Wimbledon (well, she was French, after all). Foregoing water, she was said to prefer a sip of brandy on changeovers.

Maureen Connolly

In 1953 America's 'Little Mo' became the first woman to win the calendar Grand Slam. She had won a record number of Grand Slam titles by the time she was 19, which is when, after an accident involving her horse and a lorry, she retired.

Margaret Court

Now in her seventies, Aussie Margaret Court won more Grand Slam titles than any other player in history, male or female (24 singles, 19 doubles, 21 mixed doubles). And nobody really remembers. She isn't even mentioned when talking about the best of all time. (She's 24 carat bluffing knowledge. And, uniquely, she's named after a playing area.) Note that her relative anonymity might have something to do with controversial comments she made about gay marriage. But however objectionable, they should not overshadow her remarkable achievements as a tennis player.

Billie Jean King

BJK won a hatful of majors and then started World Team Tennis, which consists of a number of teams in various US cities. She is best known for defeating 55-year-old former US number-one Bobby Riggs in a 1973 exhibition match, and being the first tennis player to come out as gay. It was a big deal in 1981.

Chris Evert

Won a whole host of majors using a two-handed backhand (a mere curiosity at the time). 'Chrissie' had the single-minded mental focus of the Terminator. She married handsome English tennis player John Lloyd in 1979, but tired of him and, instead, married handsome and charming US Olympic skier Andy Mill, but tired of him and, instead, married Andy's friend, the decidedly less-than-handsome Aussie golf player, Greg Norman. Apparently, Norman didn't cut it as a husband, either, and disappeared after a year.

Martina Navratilova

A lefty Czech defector (to the USA) who won an unrivalled number of singles, doubles and mixed doubles major titles throughout the 1970s and 1980s. At her peak, only Evert had a hope of beating her. King once said of Navratilova that she was 'the greatest singles, doubles and mixed doubles player who's ever lived'.

Steffi Graf

A German player who won 22 Grand Slam titles, she not only won the calendar Grand Slam, but also Olympic gold that same year (1988) – thus coining the term 'Golden Slam'. She is the only player to have achieved it. Graf is considered to be one of the best female players of all time. In 2001 she married Andre Agassi, the former world No. 1 who was one of the sport's most dominant players from the early 1990s to the mid-2000s. Steffi had better hair, which wasn't difficult (Andre sadly lost his).

Monica Seles

A top Yugoslav tennis player back when there was a Yugoslavia and before she became an American. She was the first of the great shriekers and hit two-handed backhands and two-handed forehands – a pioneering feat that nobody has followed. She won nine majors before her career was brought to a premature end at the age of 19 by a madman who attacked her with a knife. She survived but her tennis career sadly didn't.

Anna Kournikova

Kournikova was an average Russian pro player in the late 1990s and early 2000s. She rarely won anything but no one cared, mainly because she was strikingly attractive. The paparazzi continue to follow her in the hopes of capturing a wardrobe malfunction. Much to the disappointment of a host of male tennis fans, she has been in a relationship with Spanish crooner Enrique Iglesias for many years. She gave birth to twins in 2018. Her father Sergei is a former Greco-Roman wrestling champion.

The Williams sisters: Serena and Venus

African-American players who win a lot of Grand Slam titles – singles *and* doubles.

Serena Williams approached
the female line judge like Godzilla
approached Tokyo.

Serena, the younger sister, is the most successful female player of all time. She has the best serve ever in women's tennis. She also possesses a temper. She lost the 2009 US Open semi-final in a remarkable fashion. When serving at match point for her opponent, she was called for foot-faulting. Outraged, she approached the female line judge like Godzilla approached Tokyo, wielding the ball like a grenade and explaining: 'I swear to God, I'm f****** going to take this f****** ball and shove it down your f****** throat, you hear that? I swear to God.' Even John McEnroe went pale.

Bravely, the umpire actually penalised her a point for 'linesperson abuse'. Since it was match point, the umpire, in effect, awarded the match to her opponent (the deservedly popular eventual champion Kim Clijsters). Williams did not like the umpire's decision at all and said so. Bearing in mind her previous threat, the lineswoman is rumoured to remain in the United States Tennis Association's witness protection programme to this day.

Venus, the elder Williams sister, has won her share of major titles, designs her own tennis dresses, and tries not to upset her younger sibling.

Maria Sharapova

Another blonde Russian looker, and at one time the richest female athlete in the world. She was raised on tennis in the USA, has been ranked number one briefly on a number of separate occasions, and has a career Grand Slam to her credit. She is known primarily for her model looks and figure, steady temperament, glacial demeanour, and for shrieking really loudly every time she hits the ball. 'Masha the smasher' has earned enough money to own a successful premium chocolate and confectionery business, Sugarpova, and according to unnamed sources, much of Siberia (where she was born).

Althea Gibson

An American, Gibson was the first black woman to win a major title, the 1956 French Open. She won Wimbledon the following year. She was also a professional golfer.

THE BLUFFER'S GUIDE TO TENNIS

Ashley Harkleroad
A retired American player known for her apple-pie looks, and even better-known for her 2008 *Playboy* magazine photo spread. She attained a world ranking of 39 at the age of 18. Bluffers are guaranteed to be one step ahead of their audience should they choose to share this knowledge.

MAJOR RIVALRIES

John McEnroe and Bjorn Borg
McEnroe and Borg were like fire and ice, in that order. Mac had a tempestuous relationship with everyone and everything, including his shoes. The IceBorg, on the other hand, was cool and (at least outwardly) calm at all times. Their games were opposites as well. McEnroe's was an aggressive serve-and-volley; Borg stayed on the baseline and banged groundstrokes. Even their hair was different; Mac's was curly brown and Borg's was straight blond. Both wore headbands. They made a lovely couple.

Andre Agassi and Pete Sampras
These two are yet another backcourt specialist and serve-and-volley pair. Sampras had a tremendous serve (his second serve is considered by many to be the best ever). Agassi had, at the time, the best serve return in the game. So, things should have been pretty even? Well, yes and no. There were more fast-court majors than slow-court ones, which meant the serve-and-

volleyer had the advantage. Indeed, a good return of serve from Agassi was one that actually dribbled over the net. Pistol Pete's devastating bullet-like serve made returning more difficult than herding cats.

Jimmy Connors and Everyone

Connors was a notorious competitor. He could and would develop a powerful dislike for anyone standing on the other side of the court, ballboys included. This dislike carried over into the locker room and the tabloids as well. Regardless, excessive acrimony complemented his tennis game very nicely. And it was (and still is) widely reciprocated.

Chris Evert and Martina Navratilova

This is another rivalry of such epic proportions that you may have forgotten about the actual players. The media loved all-American 'Chrissie' but they also liked Navratilova because she defected from a communist country.

These two women had, once again, different tennis styles. Evert stayed on the baseline and rallied her opponents to death. Navratilova, not a fan of long points, charged up to the net at her earliest opportunity. Navratilova played singles and doubles; Evert liked to be the only one on her side of the court. Evert used a two-handed backhand; Navratilova used the one-handed version.

Evert and Navratilova differed in many ways aside from their tennis games. Evert was distinctly feminine, as her shapely figure and shapely legs would attest;

Navratilova was built for power. Evert was cute-looking; Navratilova had a cute personality. Evert was right-handed; not so, Navratilova. Evert was heterosexual; Navratilova was not. They took turns beating each other over the years.

Steffi Graf and Monica Seles

Graf and Seles had a great, but shortened, rivalry. Both were as tough as a cheap steak. Graf had a great forehand, as well as the best legs in tennis (that might have been mentioned before). Seles had a two-handed forehand (and backhand) and grunted a lot.

During a stretch of their rivalry, Seles won a few majors in a row and became ranked world number one. Then, a deranged fan of Graf thought that playing tennis was, in fact, a stupid way to establish a player's rank. So, in a Corleone-esque scheme to re-establish Graf as number one, he snuck up on Seles with a knife during a changeover and stabbed her in the back. Subsequently, Seles left the game for many months, lost her ranking, and never seriously challenged for the top spot again.

Roger Federer and Rafael Nadal

Rafa is Federer's biggest rival. And it's not so much about who's better. In fact, Nadal has a better head-to-head record. They are rivals in all GOAT (Greatest Of All Time) discussions. Nadal fans claim Rafa's head-to-head record with Federer is the relevant criteria. Federer fans point to who has won most majors. Discuss.

Rafael Nadal and the ATP

Rafa is always at odds with the Association of Tennis Professionals (ATP) and its individual tournaments. He and his Uncle Toni complain that all the courts on the tennis circuit are too 'fast', except, strangely enough, the French Open courts on which Rafa always wins. Nor does he like the scheduling at the US Open. And he thinks that there is too much drug testing required of the players. Other than that he's fairly undemanding.

Tim Henman and James Blake

Confound your audience by claiming that this was one of the greatest tennis rivalries that never happened. Both players reached number four in the world singles rankings without reaching the final of a Grand Slam tournament. Both were 6ft 1in right-handers known for their electric speed around the court, and for their clean-cut, affable and gentlemanly sporting personas on and off it. Hugely popular with tennis fans on both sides of the Atlantic, they were their countries' respective number ones at about the same time and, remarkably, only ever met once in a competitive match – the Tennis Masters Toronto in 2002. Tim won 6-3, 6-3. This sort of information is bluffing gold.

Incidentally, James has a British mother – which briefly made him Wimbledon's darling when he made the third round in 2006 and 2007. You might also mention that both players married beautiful blondes who are successful media professionals in their own right.

'Winning any Grand Slam tournament even once in a career is almost as rare as a polka-dot bikini on Wimbledon's Centre Court'

MAJOR MAJORS

Tennis, along with golf, and probably darts, has its major tournaments. There are four of them. Together they are called the 'Grand Slam' events which means that they're very important in the sporting calendar – not to mention as part of the bluffer's repertoire of essential tennis knowledge. The winners of the 'major' tennis tournaments are revered as heroes and enjoy legendary status for the remainder of their careers.

Incidentally, the expression 'Grand Slam' is also used when discussing the Six Nations Championship, which involves a game called rugby. If one of the six leading European rugby-playing nations (England, Wales, Scotland, Ireland, France and Italy) defeats all five of the other teams during the course of the annual championship, that nation is said to have won the 'Grand Slam'. All other similarities with professional tennis end there. (Have you ever tried playing tennis with an oval ball?)

Tennis's four major tournaments (in order of appearance) are the Australian Open, the French Open,

Wimbledon and the US Open. Tennis aficionados refer to them as 'slam' events.

By traditional definition, winning a Grand Slam means winning the Australian, the French, Wimbledon, and the US Open all in the same calendar year. Only a scant few players have been able to attain timeless glory by winning all four slams between consecutive Januarys: Don Budge, Maureen Connolly, Rod Laver (twice), Margaret Court and Steffi Graf.

Most top players don't even win a career Grand Slam – that is, winning each of these tournaments at least once in their career. The fact is that winning any of these tournaments even once in a career is almost as rare as a polka-dot bikini on Wimbledon's Centre Court.

THE AUSTRALIAN OPEN

This takes place at Melbourne Park, in January, in the city of Melbourne. Its main stadium courts are the Rod Laver (the main one), Hisense and the Margaret Court Arena. Note that the latter is never known as the Margaret Court Court (however tempting it might be to refer to it as such).

The Australian Open is called the 'friendly slam'. Not only is it fan-friendly, with an effusive and sometimes even 'bonzer' party atmosphere, it is also player-friendly – even when the players are British (the Aussies having decided that the Brits are not really worth barracking, unless they're Andy Murray – but because he's Scottish they give him a fairly easy ride).

It's summer down under in January, so the tournament is frequently played in oven-like temperatures. It can get so hot that the authorities will, as conditions merit, actually cancel play. This so scared the Australian Open officials that they constructed retractable roofs over Rod Laver and Hisense to keep the playing conditions cooler. The Margaret Court Arena, however, is open to the elements.

If you consider yourself a non-partisan moderate in all things, the Australian Open could be your proclaimed favourite slam – if you feel you need to have one. By the way, it used to be played on grass. Then, in 1988, they laid a hard court surface and decided to keep it. Rafa Nadal was a toddler at the time, and no doubt clenched a tiny fist. Bluffers should know that the current hard court is an acrylic-based tennis surface called 'plexicushion'.

THE FRENCH OPEN

The second slam of the year is the French Open. It is played in Paris at a facility known as Roland Garros, named after a dashing French aviator and World War One fighter pilot who was a keen tennis player.

The French Open is played in late May and early June. It is unique because it is the only major tournament played on slow, red clay. Fast players with strong strokes love this surface. Slow players hate it.

The French Open's slow courts add another dimension to this major event: physical fitness. Since each match for the men is best of five sets, the men need formidable reserves of physical endurance to be competitive.

The women, however, must only win two out of three sets. It could seem that the Women's Tennis Association (WTA) is acknowledging that it is the weaker sex. It's more likely, however, that they just have the more effective union. They get paid the same amount for less work; that's a remarkable deal by any negotiating standards.

If you claim to like watching long points between freakishly physically fit players, then claim the French as your favourite. Otherwise…

WIMBLEDON

The third major tournament of the year is Wimbledon, or should that be 'The Championships, Wimbledon'? No, it shouldn't. It's just Wimbledon, the oldest tennis tournament in the known universe. This major has been a fixture at the All England Lawn Tennis and Croquet Club in Wimbledon, England, since 1877. Wimbledon is now the only major tournament still played on grass (the clue's in the name of the club). Therefore, it has a faster surface than the other major tournaments. It takes a special type of player to excel on fast surfaces, and those players usually have a serve that is as hard as integral calculus. Only freaks of nature excel on both clay and grass surfaces. Borg was a freak of nature.

The All England Club takes its traditions very seriously. For instance, Wimbledon still insists that the players wear white attire (*see* page 21). The other majors let them wear pretty much any mismatched shirt and shorts they can piece together after an overnight drunken charity shop fest.

In fact, tradition is a tradition at Wimbledon. Whatever was, still is. Moreover, Wimbledon is the most popular slam among the players and actual tennis fans.

When asked why it is their favourite, they agree: it's 'because of the tradition'.

However, in the interest of fairness, an occasional tradition has been scrapped. Example: Wimbledon now seeds its players using the current world rankings. Until a few years ago, the tournament seeded the players based on their grass-court play prowess. The clay-courters protested against this method because they were being regularly and routinely thrown to the serve-and-volley players like pork chops to Rottweilers. Obviously, early tournament exits meant less prize money. You can see their point.

Only freaks of nature excel on both clay and grass surfaces.

Wimbledon holds the record for the longest match ever held in professional competition. In 2010, the then-world-number-23, American John Isner, defeated the unseeded French qualifier Nicolas Mahut 6-4, 3-6, 6-7 (7-9), 7-6 (7-3), 70-68. The match took three days (over 11 hours) to complete, and became a persuasive argument for the introduction of a fifth-set tiebreaker. Stop press! Now there is. Remarkably, Isner was involved in yet another marathon match in the 2018 semi-final against South African player Kevin Anderson, who beat him 26-24 in a final set which lasted nearly three hours. The club bowed to pressure from players and coaches (but not media organisations or fans) and introduced a final set tiebreak which takes effect when the score reaches 12-12.

THE US OPEN

The fourth and final major is played at the National Tennis Center in Flushing Meadows in New York City and takes place in late August and early September.

The US Open is the 'maverick slam', the antithesis of Wimbledon, in the sense that anything goes. The only tradition there is that there is no tradition. Players can wear whatever they want and can even enter and leave the court to music. One memorable night, when Federer was world number one and in his prime, he entered the court to Darth Vader's theme from *Star Wars*.

The US Open spectators can get a tad rowdy (*see* 'Spectator etiquette', opposite). New Yorkers refuse to adhere to normal rules of etiquette. They can be quite loud at inappropriate moments and, in fact, are quite proud of their brash insolence.

The US Open stadium courts are named after a couple of American legends: Arthur Ashe (the main court) and Louis Armstrong. Nobody's quite sure of the relevance of the latter, other than that he was a great jazz musician.

In short, the US Open can be described as 'raucous'. With crowds regularly becoming rather excitable and rock music issuing from the grounds' speakers, and with the nearby LaGuardia airport's passenger jets within reach of a badly aimed overhead slam, it's certainly a different kind of major tennis tournament.

Note that it used to be played on grass. At some point, the organisers realised that grass was a very traditional playing surface. So, they changed it to clay. That solved that problem. But then they realised no American grew up playing on clay. 'What were we thinking?' they asked each other in disbelief. So, they changed it again to a hard court version. Now it is played on something called DecoTurf. (Note that Connors is the only player to have won the tournament on all three of those surfaces – grass, clay and hard court).

SPECTATOR ETIQUETTE

Tennis spectators are generally imagined to be a mild-mannered group of polite enthusiasts who attend important matches, speak only in hushed whispers and intersperse the play with polite applause. The reality is rather different.

Typically, the crowds that attend professional tennis tournaments are a combination of diehard fans, hobbyists, an aspiring bluffer or two, and…foreigners. Yes, no matter what country the tournament is played in, and no matter what country a player hails from, dozens of expatriate supporters not only attend their player's matches, but paint their faces and/or chests in the colours of that player's country's flag. They also relentlessly wave their home country's flag and yell cryptic, patriotic slogans such as: 'Aussie, Aussie, Aussie. Oy, oy, oy!'

As absurd as this may sound, it's just good, clean (except for the paint) fun. Other partisan sections of the crowd can be negatively intrusive, and these are more likely to be 'home' fans. They will frequently be guilty of employing unsportsmanlike tactics to support their player, such as barking out random noises just as the opponent performs his or her service toss. As a good bluffer, you should not condone this boorish behaviour – certainly not while sober.

RULES FOR SPECTATING

While attending an actual match, it's good to know at least the basic protocol that spectators at a tennis match are expected to follow. The primary rule is simple: do what the others are doing. If they clap, you clap. If they groan, you groan. If they offer to buy you a drink, you offer to drink it.

There are a few 'don'ts' to keep in mind and even complain about during spectating – mainly speaking above a whisper or moving around during points. In the same vein, those spectators who cough, shout to friends or suffer intrusive heart attacks during points are poor sportsmen. Be sure to mock them roundly in public.

Advanced spectator action points for bluffers to master are as follows:

Common applause points include:
* your preferred player's entrance onto the court;
* any player's service aces (exuberant or mild applause, depending);
* any player's winners (exuberant or mild as above);
* excellent tries and efforts;
* excellent gets and saves (withheld until after the point is over);
* exceedingly long points;
* end of a set;
* any show of sportsmanship (rare);

* end of the match; and
* as players walk off the court.

Common groan and audible sigh points:
* A net ball goes over the net.
* A ball clearly lands 'out' but the chronically myopic line judge calls it 'in'.
* A player falls over.
* A spectator tries to disturb the opposing player by yelling at crucial moments.
* A player argues with the umpire.
* A player is struck in a sensitive part of the anatomy by the ball.
* The game is suspended for rain/bad light/nuclear war.

Common jeer points:
* The opposing player smashes his or her racquet/has a tantrum.
* The opposing player takes a medical time out (MTO) as a disruptive ploy.
* A player threatens a line judge, umpire, ballgirl, etc., with a dirty look, etc.
* A player has the temerity to criticise a spectator or, worse, the entire crowd.
* A player refuses to bow or curtsey to the Royal Box at Wimbledon.
* Sir Cliff Richard stands up to sing.

DRESS CODE
There isn't one, generally speaking. Although at Wimbledon umbrellas are a compulsory accessory.

The most uncoordinated player at the club, the 'club stalwart' subscribes to every tennis magazine and has taken hundreds of tennis lessons, yet is still on the bottom rung of the ladder.

ON THE LEVEL

Competition occurs at every level of tennis. At the club level, competition is vigorously encouraged. Clubs even organise a 'ladder' in order to humiliate everyone not at the top of it into challenging for greater things. This challenging system initiates all sorts of interactions along the lines of:

Challenger I'm challenging you, Merv; is Monday okay for you?

Merv I'm sorry, I'll be in the Cayman Islands for a month attending to my tax shelters.

Club challenges are issued all the time, and dodged just as frequently. If you're on a ladder, take every opportunity to complain vociferously about how players on higher rungs than you keep avoiding your perfectly reasonable challenges.

ESTABLISHING YOUR LEVEL

You need to have a playing level. There are a number of ways people calculate a level, but you don't need to worry about that. Just concentrate instead on the International Tennis Number or 'ITN' which categorises players like entomologists categorise beetles. The rankings are numbered 1 to 10. But instead of 10 being the best, like Bo Derek, 10 is the worst (typical of tennis's track record on scoring anything sensibly). Just the same, here are the ratings (with helpful explanations):

ITN 10

Starting to play competitively (can serve, rally and score) on full court using a regular yellow ball. (First lesson: never play with balls in any colour other than yellow; it's bluffing suicide.)

ITN 9

Needs on-court experience, though strokes can be completed with some success. (He or she can hit the ball about as often as a comet flies past.)

ITN 8

Able to judge/control where the ball is going and can sustain a short rally. (Yeah, maybe two shots in a row.)

ITN 7

Fairly consistent when hitting medium-paced shots, but is not yet comfortable with all the strokes. This player lacks control over depth, direction and power. (This player still has a very long way to go.)

ITN 6

Exhibits more aggressive net play, has improved court coverage, improved shot control and is developing teamwork in doubles. (This is the minimum rating you should claim. It suggests you may be able to play tennis.)

ITN 5

Has dependable strokes, including directional control and depth on both groundstrokes and moderate shots. The player has the ability to use lobs, overheads, approach shots and volleys with some success. (This is another rating the bluffer could claim. It includes all the shots. You can say modestly that you probably don't deserve it, which of course will most likely be true.)

> Never play with balls in any
> colour other than yellow;
> it's bluffing suicide.

ITN 4

Can use power and spins and has begun to handle pace. He or she has sound footwork, can control depth of shots and can vary game plans according to opponents. The player can hit first serves with power and second serves with spin. (You can claim this level at a pinch, but just pray to God you're never called upon to prove it.)

ITN 3

Has good shot control and frequently has an outstanding shot or attribute around which a game may be structured. The player can regularly hit winners and force errors off short balls, can put away volleys and overheads, and has a variety of serves. (You're probably the best player in your club. You could have been a contender if you were remotely bothered. You don't need to bluff.)

ITN 2

Has power/consistency as a major weapon. He or she can vary strategies and styles of play in a competitive situation. This player is usually nationally ranked. (It does depend on where you live, though. If you live in Mauritania you would be nationally ranked. If you live in Florida you probably wouldn't.)

ITN 1

This player has had intensive training for national tournament competitions at the junior and senior levels and has extensive professional tournament experience. Currently holds or is capable of holding an ATP/WTA ranking and their major source of income is through tournament prize money. (These players can do with tennis balls what Shakespeare could do with English.)

In summary:

ITN numbers 1 through 4 are very accomplished players. They get asked to play a lot and are also asked deep tennis questions like, 'Who won Indian Wells?' Or, 'What's Andy Murray's middle name?' Don't claim to be among them.

ITN numbers 7 through 10 aren't much good. Don't ever admit that they're too good for you.

Bluffers should never be higher than a 5 or lower than a 6. By now you will have enough tennis knowledge to converse intelligently without having to know enough to be asked to coach or, more importantly, demonstrate.

What you now need to know, most importantly, is who's who at your local club (or court).

CLUB TYPES

The make-up of members of a club is diverse, yet predictable. It seems almost Darwinian in the way each niche is filled. The following list, like every other in this slim volume, does not set out to be comprehensive, but many of the types described will be instantly recognisable. One of them is also likely to be you.

The Carper

There's always one. She complains that there are not enough social events. She complains that there should be more children's clinics. She complains that too many children are using the courts. She complains that nobody asks her to play.

The Fossil

He hasn't actually played since men wore white flannels. Still, he shows up every day, watches matches, picks up litter, and hoarsely yells at the myriad mindless kids running around having fun.

The Cougar

She plays tennis in full make-up, wearing two pounds of jewellery. She has enough gold chain to shackle the men's singles champion to a tree and devour him. She only plays doubles because covering a singles court would sap her energy for the real purpose of her presence at the club.

The Dragon

She is very athletic and one of the best players at the club. She prefers to wear shorts and can bench-press her own body weight. She is also tactless, opinionated and constantly speaks her mind. When she's angry her breath can burn toast from 200 yards. It's her opinion that the best way to end a point (and possibly a match) is to smack the ball squarely into one of her opponent's vital organs.

The Eco-bore

He pickets club meetings with placards demanding separate glass, aluminium, plastic, paper and styrofoam recycle bins on every court. He rides his bike all around town and puts flyers on cars encouraging drivers to carpool to the club for the sake of the baby frogs.

The Sycophant

She gushes over the head pro, the assistant pro, the club secretary, the assistant secretary, the number-one male player, the number-one female player, the club prodigy and any member who's a lawyer, doctor or investment banker. She pointedly ignores everybody else.

The Jock
He played rugby at university and has now taken up tennis, signing up for a year's worth of lessons. He watches the pros on TV but unfortunately the only thing he has learned is that pros hit the ball harder than club players. Not one to settle for second best, he emulates the pros. He believes that one day the shots he drives through the chain-link fence will begin to land in the court. He likes towelling off, drinking his sports liquid and snacking on an energy bar, and he tends to wander around the changing room naked. Because he's a jock.

The Chairperson
She is the perennial club president, captain of the women's team, membership committee chairperson and social committee chairperson. With her club positions and her regular job as the manager of a catering staff company, she seldom actually gets to play tennis.

The Stud
He is suave, sophisticated and successful. He drives a convertible Jag which he parks in two spaces, and wears Ray-Bans. The ladies all strive to catch his eye. He strives to avoid catching the cougar's eye. Aspiring studs all strive to catch a cast-off or two. He scores far better with female members than he does on the tennis court.

The Chauvinist
The dominant male chauvinist is the best source of dirty jokes in the club bar. He took up tennis because the women wear such short skirts. He enjoys innuendos on and off

THE BLUFFER'S GUIDE TO TENNIS

the court. When not playing tennis, he likes to sit around watching the women's doubles. He is prone to drooling.

The Fat Cat

A self-made millionaire, he lives in a mansion and has a tennis court next to his pool. He always talks in business jargon. Phrases like 'buy third-quarter market indicators constraining amortisation of the long-term fiscal debt' roll off his tongue while his fellow players go broke misinterpreting his advice.

The Bigot

An ultra-conservative, he lives behind a 10-foot-high razor-wire fence in a house he has wittily named Whitehaven. He preaches that the government is disincentivising the poor with overgenerous welfare payments. He still plays in all-white clothes, and believes there is a United Nations conspiracy to introduce a quota of black players into club locker rooms.

The Psycho

She has a hair-trigger temper, and regularly turns red, curses, and smashes her racquet into non-composite fibres when she plays poorly, which she loosely defines as 'missing a shot'. The members are frightened to play with her but they fear she'll blow up the ball machine if they refuse.

The Secretary

She looks like she could body slam a Coke machine. She makes sure the subs come in on time and that guests have paid. To say she is a cross between Genghis Khan and the president of the National Organisation of Ball-breakers is being charitable.

The Analyst
He doesn't take lessons. Instead, he imitates the strokes of one or more of the top five players in the world today. After a world rankings change, he will explain why it has happened and offer an exhaustive exposition of where a top professional is going wrong.

The Prodigy
His parents take him to a big-name pro at another club and to play in tournaments in neighbouring counties. The members agree that this kid has the ability to be a top pro some day, especially if his more antisocial tendencies – like arson and drilling spyholes in the women's changing room – are disregarded.

The Walter Mitty
Rarely seen away from the bar, his life reads like a Russian novel. He has endless war stories and has had more sexual adventures than Christian Grey. He also delights club members with interesting and humorous accounts of every match he's ever played.

The Stalwart
The most uncoordinated player at the club, he subscribes to every tennis magazine and has taken hundreds of tennis lessons, yet is still on the bottom rung of the ladder. However, he loves tennis and gets more pure enjoyment out of it than anyone else at the club.

The Radical

Politically she is to the left of Stalin. She distrusts all businesses and corporations, but especially 'Big Tennis'. She wants the government to take over and regulate all tennis clubs 'so the homeless can join'. She advocates government-subsidised catering, free board for welfare claimants, free gut string and free lessons.

The Hypochondriac

He is suffering from an acute case of terminal tennis elbow. He ices, heats, wraps, braces and spreads athletic cream on his tortured humerus before and after playing tennis, and then regales fellow members with stories about what else he's suffering from.

The Genius

He knows all sorts of fascinating things, like how flies land upside down on the ceiling, origami, the atomic weight of thorium and Alexander the Great's last name. He has a PhD in some obscure field like comparative invertebrate mathematics. The only subjects that stump him are women, fashion and tennis.

The Uber-competitor

A very serious and intense person, she competes at everything – even coupon clipping. She is deeply offended when she loses the racquet spin. However, she usually wins her matches because everyone she plays either plays for fun or would feel guilty if she went broke paying for a therapist.

The Hustler

He likes to make things 'interesting'. He plays like a comatose zombie if no one will bet with him. But given a wager, he springs to life like a just-paid sailor on shore leave.

The Brewmeister

He never plays without a six-pack of beer on the court. Nor does he sit down without a beer in his hand. His tennis isn't so hot. But then, who cares? He's never at a loss for people to play with because he always shares his beer.

The Vamp

Guys line the club entrance when she drives up, and jockey for the adjacent courts when she plays tennis in her sports bra and spandex shorts. Although she doesn't play tennis particularly well, she remains the club's most popular mixed-doubles partner.

Balls don't bounce off fast courts; they skid – low and hard. That means balls must be scraped off the court surface like chewing gum. Very irritating.

ON THE SURFACE

Over the years, tennis authorities have tried many different kinds of materials on which to play tennis. Some materials have proven to be monumental failures. Gravel, ice, plastic, linoleum, PVC, vinyl, brick, slate, concrete, tarmac and wood all failed to make the grade. The tennis powers eventually settled on a few tried-and-tested surfaces. It will depend on things such as geography, budget and politics to explain those preferred in the area where you choose to watch or play your tennis.

GRASS

Grass used to be the most common court surface. In fact, a few short decades ago, along with jolly old Wimbledon, the US Open and the Australian Open were both played on grass. Now it is in danger of becoming obsolete. Only about 10 per cent of all top pro matches are now contested on grass, and those professionals who modify their game for playing on more widespread surfaces hardly surprisingly find themselves out of sorts on grass courts. Ever wondered why Nadal tends to struggle at Wimbledon, while Federer can cruise to the semi-finals without dropping a set?

Grass is a bona fide fast surface and fast courts are annoying. Balls don't bounce off fast courts; they skid – low and hard. That means balls must be scraped off the court surface like chewing gum. Very irritating.

If you regularly play on nice, normal-surfaced courts and then, due to a sudden brain spasm, decide to play on a fast one, you are guaranteed to look and hit like a complete novice. You will be hitting balls into the nets of the adjacent courts, if you're lucky. Frequently, the ball will go scooting under your racquet like a cockroach late for curfew.

So, instead of having everybody wait patiently for the ball to bounce up like an inviting dust bunny, the ball skips off the grass low and quick. Therefore, it's a surface that's made to order for players with big 120mph-plus serves. The players themselves don't have to be particularly fast. They typically hit their meteoric serves and then lumber into the net where they volley away the feeble return for a winner. It's not exactly a gripping spectacle.

There are currently only a relative handful of pro-tournament grass courts left around the world. Most of them are in south-west London. If the groundskeepers went on strike in Wimbledon, there would be no tournament. Anyway, that's not really the point. The point is that as players were hitting the ball harder and faster on grass surfaces, people started to notice that serves weren't being returned nearly as often, which resulted in stupefyingly boring tennis games of the sort championed by Pat Rafter, Andy Roddick and Pete Sampras. Great guys, no doubt, but nobody ever said they provided riveting entertainment. So, Wimbledon got world-renowned grass experts to slow down its courts so that clay-court specialists could use their much-vaunted foot speed to run down shots with relish. Crowds were thrilled and, with all that extra time on their hands, immediately began consuming vast quantities of strawberries and cream in their excitement – which was probably always the intention.

> The majority of clay courts
> play slower than a week spent
> watching grass grow.

CLAY

Clay courts play the opposite of grass ones. The balls bounce up higher on clay so that any squirrelly (small and fast) player can smugly smack back even the hardest of shots.

Even so, there are clay courts that actually play fast. The tournament in Barcelona, Spain, for example, is held on surfaces that play very fast. Therefore, the dedicated clay-court specialists despise it and threaten it with faux muscle pulls and/or absenteeism.

Yes, it allows the slower hard hitters to compete with them on their surface. However, the majority of clay courts play slower than a week spent watching grass grow. They are so slow that lectures on plant photosynthesis seem to fly by like pheromone-crazed hornets.

There are a couple of things that you can say distinguish clay courts from the other types:

> Players can 'slide' and 'skate' to the ball and then hit it. On the other surfaces, sliding tends to roll the players' ankles over like a fallow deer on skates.

> Balls leave marks when they bounce on these courts. You don't need to be Sherlock Holmes to determine whether a ball landed in or out. Regardless, arguments may still ensue.

HARD COURTS

Hard courts are all the other kinds of courts, including acrylic carpets. Hard courts are not fast; nor are they slow. They are somewhere in between. Still, the tennis powers tweak and notch up their speeds like an obsessive F1 pit crew. Consequently, the hard courts of the Australian Open tend to be slower than those of the US Open.

Hard courts can be painted all sorts of unusual colours: red and green, blue and green, blue and a lighter blue. The list is endless. Design consultants have been called in to help make courts more pleasing to the eye, and in some more enlightened and liberal countries like the Democratic People's Republic of Korea (that would be the northern non-democratic part), they have them in the colours of the national flag, with a red star at each end and the tramlines in a fetching shade of blue.

In Madrid they came up with unnaturally fast and unnaturally blue clay courts. The clay-court specialists hated that they were 'fast', but also blamed the courts' blueness which was intended to aid visibility (for TV viewers). They were soon banned.

ASPHALT

Finally, there exists a completely ghastly and hideous bitumen-based tennis court substance known as asphalt or the 'black death'. Nobody can be exactly sure how prevalent this abomination is across the globe, but you can bet your life it's big in downtown Pyongyang. After only a few shots on an asphalt court, a player's hands and the ball turns black.

Most civilised cities have strict ordinances which restrict asphalt to the streets where it belongs. Unfortunately, some misguided and ignorant communities have constructed tennis courts with this toxic substance. As a bluffer you will be in good company abhorring them.

There's no point in pretending that you know everything about tennis – nobody does – but if you've got this far and you've absorbed at least a modicum of the information and advice contained within these pages, then you will almost certainly know more than 99% of the rest of the human race about what tennis is, who plays it, where they play it, and why. You will also know a fair bit about how to play it, and certainly enough to converse knowledgeably with people who do it for a living.

What you now do with this information is up to you, but here's a suggestion: be confident about your newfound knowledge, see how far it takes you, but above all have fun using it. You are now a bona fide expert in the art of bluffing about one of the world's oldest and most keenly contested racquet sports. And bear in mind that the only bluffing skill you really need to master is to talk a good game – while avoiding anything that might actually involve attempting to play it. That's never a good idea.

GLOSSARY

Ace To serve a ball that not only cannot be returned, it cannot be touched.

Athena Tennis Girl Iconic bestselling poster depicting a nubile young woman hitching up a short tennis dress and rubbing her naked bottom. The model, Fiona Walker, was an art student in Birmingham where the image was captured in 1976, thus bringing the story of tennis full circle (see page 7). The dress (naturally pristine white) is now on display at the Wimbledon Museum Collection.

Baseline Its precise position is much disputed when a ball lands anywhere near it.

Charting A means of statistically evaluating your game. Always useful to drop into conversation, as in: '77.23% of my drop shots are winners.' With luck, your opponent will believe this and spend most of the time at the net, while you blithely hit winner after winner into the back of the court.

Choke The term used to describe what happens to competitors whose elbows fuse at a 90-degree angle during important points.

Club pro A person who teaches tennis for large sums of money by making pupils run around all over the court while telling them what they're doing wrong – then making them pick up the balls.

Cross-court A shot that is hit from one side of the court to the other.

Double fault Missing two serves in a row. That's nobody's fault but your own.

Doubles When two people play against two other people. They don't have to be of the same gender.

Down the line A shot aimed parallel to one of the side lines, which, ideally, you'll want it to land inside. If the ball's clearly heading out, your only hope is for your myopic opponent to assume it's staying in, lunge for it, and help it on its way. Generally speaking, it's much safer to hit the ball cross-court. It's a bigger target area.

Drop shot A shot used by players to demonstrate their out-and-out contempt for cowardly baseliner opponents.

Fast court A court that allows the ball to skid fast and low under your racquet head.

Fault A missed serve.

Foot fault Stepping on or across the baseline before you hit your serve. Never a good idea to accuse Serena Williams of being guilty of one.

Forced error When your opponent's shot is so good that it makes you miss your shot. In other words, it's not your fault.

Forehand To hit the ball on your dominant side of the body. The world's easiest tennis shot.

Gamesmanship Not quite cheating, but not far off.

Grand Slam Winning the Australian Open, French

Open, Wimbledon and US Open all in one calendar year. Holding all four titles over two years is considered more of a 'slam'.

Hacker A person with no tennis sense, knowledge or ability, but who owns a racquet.

Half-volley A shot hit immediately after the bounce, or one you hit when you can't think of any other sort.

Hobbyist An occasional tennis player who doesn't do drills or work out unless the aerobics instructor is 'hot'.

Let When a server hits the net and the ball lands 'in', a 'let' is played and the serve is taken again. The word is derived either from the French *filet* (for net) or the Olde English word *lettan* (to hinder). Bluffers should go with the latter.

Line judge A trained expert in the Science of Bounced Balls.

Lob A high, soft shot, guaranteed to delight your opponent.

Lob volley An improbable winner.

Mine Doubles code word for 'I can't miss!'

Net The place that exercises a magnetic attraction over fuzzy, yellow, round objects.

Oh and oh A term used by winners to relate their match score of 6-0, 6-0. ('Oh and oh' losers never give the score; in fact, they won't acknowledge that the match ever took place.)

On serve Neither player can get a lead of more than one game. Tiebreaker ahead.

On the rise When you are late for your half-volley.

Out A ball that lands outside the lines, or what a player yells when a point is needed.

Overhead The easiest way to hit yourself on the head with a tennis ball.

'Play two' What you bellow when a ball rolls onto your court as your opponent is about to slam your short lob away.

Poach Doubles term. When the net man or woman intercepts his or her opponents' service return. It shows your utter contempt for your opponents.

Put-away Hitting a winner with disdain.

Quick serve The one you hit while your opponent is tying his/her shoelaces.

Rally To hit balls back and forth over the net without keeping score.

Real tennis Curious version of the game which enthusiasts claim to be the inspiration behind lawn tennis. It is played indoors in specially built courts (of which there are only about 40 around the world), and the ball is allowed to bounce off walls. Apparently King Henry VIII was a keen player. Probably better to describe it as 'surreal tennis'.

Return of serve The shot that hits serves back and brings on those feelings of dread when you realise you have to serve again.

Seed A player you don't mind losing to in a tournament.

Slow court What you call a court when you lose because your opponent kept hitting all your shots back.

Spin To make the ball rotate; and what real players apply on purpose.

Split step A technique used to step in two opposite directions at the same time. Not recommended.

Sweet spot The centre part of the strings of your racquet where striking the ball gives it the best chance of going where you intended it. The larger the better, but never admit to that being a consideration – because, naturally, you always hit the ball dead centre anyway.

Switch Doubles code word for 'Let's trade places.' Or, 'Quick, let's hide my backhand.'

'These go' To let your opponent know you're ready to keep score according to your rules.

Tiebreaker That part of the match where the most chokes occur.

Tournament A place where you pay money to play someone who wouldn't otherwise be caught dead on the same court with you.

Umpire A figure of authority who sits in a high chair above your court and makes players play by the rules.

Unforced error When you miss your shot for no reason, or because of diabolically powerful and invisible forces such as: a) your strings were not spaced evenly; or b) your dog ate your lucky socks.

Wings What Aussies call stroke sides. They say 'forehand wing' and 'backhand wing'. This terminology is working its way through some American tennis announcers. Use the term. You will definitely sound not only tennis smart, but you will also demonstrate your global tennis awareness.

Winner An 'in' shot that an opponent can't touch.

Yours Doubles code word for 'You can take the blame for missing that.'

Zoned A term referring to the fact that for some inexplicable reason your shots keep landing in the court and passing your opponent.

A BIT MORE BLUFFING...

Bluffer's GUIDE TO BREXIT
Bluffer's GUIDE TO CRICKET
Bluffer's GUIDE TO MANAGEMENT
Bluffer's GUIDE TO CYCLING
Bluffer's GUIDE TO SOCIAL MEDIA
Bluffer's GUIDE TO ETIQUETTE
Bluffer's GUIDE TO RACING
Bluffer's GUIDE TO GOLF
Bluffer's GUIDE TO WINE
Bluffer's GUIDE TO JAZZ
Bluffer's GUIDE TO DOGS
Bluffer's GUIDE TO FISHING
Bluffer's GUIDE TO OPERA
Bluffer's GUIDE TO CHOCOLATE
Bluffer's GUIDE TO CATS
Bluffer's GUIDE TO BEER
Bluffer's GUIDE TO QUANTUM UNIVERSE
Bluffer's GUIDE TO FOOTBALL
Bluffer's GUIDE TO RUGBY
Bluffer's GUIDE TO SKIING
Bluffer's GUIDE TO SEX
Bluffer's GUIDE TO HOLLYWOOD
Bluffer's GUIDE TO POETRY
Bluffer's GUIDE TO JOURNALISM
Bluffer's GUIDE TO PUBLIC RELATIONS
Bluffer's GUIDE TO FORMULA 1
Bluffer's GUIDE TO SURFING
Bluffer's GUIDE TO HIKING
Bluffer's GUIDE TO TENNIS

Available from all good bookshops

bluffers.com